WITHDRAWN
L. R. COLLEGE LIBRARY

San Carlos Borremeo de Carmelo, Carmel, California
(photo by Lee Blaisdell—Monterey Studio)

it afforded protection to both the Indians and the Spaniards who were fleeing New Mexico pueblos after the barbaric Indian Revolt of 1680, led by Popé.

The Mission is closely tied to the history of the Tiguas Indians, who are the oldest permanent settlers of the State of Texas. This ancient mission has survived flood, storm, and partial destruction by fire. After the fire of 1907 it was rebuilt with the original sacristy walls, which had remained intact. It stands today, in much of its ancient glory, near the town of Ysleta, and its farm has been cultivated continuously since 1682. The Mission and the farm are now operated by the Jesuit Fathers.

ARIZONA

The territory of what is now the State of Arizona lay between two extensive missionary areas, those of New Mexico and California. It boasts but five missions to the Indians in the seventeenth and eighteenth centuries. The one that remains is considered a beauty and is called by the Indians, "La Paloma Blanca del Desierto" (White Dove of the Desert).

This mission, named San Xavier del Bac, is situated on an elevation in the Santa Cruz valley nine miles south of the city of Tucson. It is a bright oasis against the dun colors of the desert and the dusty green of mesquite and sage. The name is derived from the early Indian settlement called "Bac," the place where the waters appear, because the Santa Cruz river which ran underground for some distance reappeared on the surface nearby.

The first missionary to visit this territory was the Jesuit explorer, Father Eusebio Francisco Kino, in 1692. At that time the Sobaipuri Indians inhabited the fertile lands, but these people were later supplanted by Papagos from the desert lands to the west.

*San Carlos Borremeo de Carmelo, Carmel, California
(photo by Lee Blaisdell—Monterey Studio)*

The foundations of the first church were laid by Father Kino in 1700, about two miles distant from the site of the present Mission. He named it after the famed Jesuit "Apostle to the Indies," St. Francis Xavier. The present church of San Xavier was built by Fathers Baltazar Carrillo and Narcisco Gutierrez, under the expert direction of the architect and builder Ignacio Gaona. This building, the result of fourteen years' work, was completed in 1797.

The Mission of San Xavier is acclaimed the finest example of mission architecture in the United States. The term mission architecture may be defined as the Spanish-colonial style of Mexico, modified by the limitations of local material and adapted by the capabilities of available artisans. The Mission is late Renaissance of Mexico, evincing the influence of the derivative styles of Moorish and Byzantine. The best view can be had from some distance in front of the church; from here is seen the facade of ornamental detail above the entrance, which is flanked by terraced towers. Between the towers rises a majestic dome, the most outstanding, perhaps, in American mission architecture.

The interior of the church is approached through weathered doors of mesquite. These give entry into a vaulted area which serves as a form of vestibule opening directly onto the nave. The church is of burned brick covered with lime plaster, and measures ninety-eight-and-a-half feet long. The walls have an average thickness of three feet except at the base of the towers where, in order to carry the great weight, they are nearly six feet in width. The form is that of the Latin cross, with nave, transept, and apse outlining the form. It should be remembered that in addition to the religious purpose of these missions they were constructed to serve also as stations of defense.

The builder of San Xavier del Bac added a grace note of humor to the superb design of the façade. Clinging to the

Old Chapel, Bethlehem, Pennsylvania (photo by Carroll Tobias)

inner curves of the lower volutes are a cat and mouse carved in full relief. Across the breadth of the gable they glare at each other with relentless suspicion. May they long continue to do so, for the Indians of San Xavier say, "When cat catches mouse, end of world will come."

CALIFORNIA

The known history of the famous missions of California, twenty-one of them stretching northward up the Pacific coast along El Camino Real, begins as early as 1493 with the papal decision of Pope Alexander VI, which divided the newly-explored round world into two hemispheres with the title to all land discovered east of the dividing line going to Portugal and in the west going to Spain. But the successful chain of churches and ranchos of the Spaniards had its beginning in the summer of 1769, when Franciscan Padre Junípero Serra established the first California Mission. From this point, missionary activity, like a Christian banner, rippled north-ward up the coast. This movement was also to have great extra-religious significance, not the least aspect of which was that the presence of these Spanish missions was to deter the Russians from getting a too-firm foothold on our western coast.

A period of great effort preceded the founding of these mission churches. Spain, after discovery of the West, had been granted by the reigning Pontiff the right of exploration and development of the new western lands. Slow transport and rugged countryside made the going difficult, but the mission-aries persevered. So, unfortunately, did the free-booters and adventurers who turned their energies to exploiting the new land.

The need for regulation was recognized by Spain's Charles I, who decreed as early as Cortés' conquest of Mexico that

opposite: Green Bay East Moravian Church, Green Bay, Wisconsin (photo by Clement E. Suemper)

Indians were not to be held as slaves, but were to be paid wages. While other laws to encourage and protect the Indians were later passed, and frequently re-stated, enforcement was difficult. Active concern for the welfare of the Indians was fairly well limited to the missions. Here the natives were converted, schooled, and protected from the injustices which were rampant beyond mission boundaries.

When the Spanish took over control of the coast, the start was made in Guatemala to the south and reached northward. But the Spaniards were vacillating in their policies, and their world power was in decline. When finally the Franciscans began their building to secure the missions, a final effort was being made to secure California as a land for colonization and to effect the reestablishment of Spain as a dominant power among the nations of the world. But the sea power of Spain was lost; England was victorious in Canada; America became independent; Napoleon disrupted Spain's home rule; and the Russians were coming down from the north—seeking a foothold they were never to achieve. Indeed, the missions were built against a swiftly changing background in these years from 1769 to 1823.

Early arrivals from Lower California, that peninsula which lies to the south of the State and is now a part of Mexico, were Father Junípero Serra and Don Gaspar de Portolá, who came near to what is now San Diego. There, by the seashore, they erected a brushwood shelter which in July, 1769, became Father Serra's first church in California. Later a permanent structure, San Diego de Alcalá, was built. There followed an intensive program of mission building which spans only fifty-four years but constitutes an impressive record even from the standpoint of construction alone. Twenty-one of these missions remain as churches to the present day. Here they are, in the sequence of their founding dates.

Holy Name of Mary Church, Sault Ste. Marie, Michigan
(Beauchamp's Studio)

1. San Diego de Alcalá—July 16, 1769
2. San Carlos Borromeo—June 3, 1770
3. San Antonio de Padua—July 14, 1771
4. San Gabriel Arcángel—September 8, 1771
5. San Luis Obispo de Tolosa—September 1, 1772
6. San Francisco de Asís—October 9, 1776
7. San Juan Capistrano—November 1, 1776
8. Santa Clara de Asís—January 12, 1777
9. San Buenaventura—March 31, 1782
10. Santa Bárbara—December 4, 1786
11. La Purísima Concepción—December 8, 1787
12. Santa Cruz—September 25, 1791
13. Nuestra Señora de la Soledad—October 9, 1791
14. San José de la Guadalupe—June 1, 1797
15. San Juan Bautista—June 24, 1797
16. San Miguel Arcángel—July 25, 1797
17. San Fernando Rey de España—September 8, 1797
18. San Luis Rey de Francia—June 13, 1798
19. Santa Inés—September 17, 1804
20. San Rafael Arcángel—December 14, 1817
21. San Francisco de Solano—July 4, 1823

Some among these twenty-one have been greatly restored even to details, and all continue to serve the greater purpose of their construction.

We select but one for detailed treatment, because it is a memorial in a special sense to Father Junípero Serra, and was the designated head of the chain of missions he established. This is the Mission San Carlos Borromeo de Carmelo at Carmel-by-the-sea in California. The Mission was founded June 3, 1770, by Father Serra, who had arrived at Monterey from Lower California early that same year.

The present stone church was built by Father Lasuen in 1793, after Serra's death. In 1824 the Mission was secularized, falling into decay along with the other buildings of the quadrangle. The work of restoring this historic landmark was undertaken in 1884 by Father Angelo Casanova, and the reconditioning continues. Here are kept many relics of the early days: the kitchen cooking utensils, the original vestments, the books of the first library in California, and articles of the Mission period.

The Shrine of the Blessed Mother at the Mission has a history of its own. Devotion to Our Lady of Bethlehem dates back to the fifteenth century. She was venerated in a small chapel located at Restelo near Lisbon, Portugal, which became a center of devotion of navigators and sailors. After two hundred and twenty-seven years of exploration and colonization in the New World, Spain, aware of the encroachment of the Russians from the north, made plans to guard the northern frontiers of the colonies by taking possession of California land to the north. The Archbishop of Mexico City, the Most Reverend Francisco de Lorenzaña, gave to the expedition to Monterey a beautiful statue of Our Lady of Bethlehem to represent the Conquistadora of this new land. When the Mission was abandoned, after secularization, the image of Our Lady of Bethlehem was cared for by the last Indian family to remain at the Mission. Dona Ignacia, the daughter of this family, became custodian of the statue, and when she took up residence in Monterey, she enshrined it in her home. Just before her death she requested that the statue be given to Gertrude Ambrosia, a descendant of one of the soldiers who had accompanied Father Serra. It was she who in 1948 returned the statue to the restored Mission church.

WESTWARD EXPANSION

The expansion of denominations by missionary effort was relatively fast. In the first fifty years of the nineteenth century, in the aftermath of the Revolution, there was a great wave of immigration, and the swelling population streamed inland. In 1776, for example, the Congregational churches had been concentrated heavily in Connecticut, Massachusetts, Rhode Island, Vermont, New Hampshire, and Maine, but there were few in New York State, only one in New Jersey, two in South Carolina, and one in Georgia. By 1860, Congregationalism had spread almost in a straight line westward from New York as far as Minnesota, Iowa, and Kansas, and then, with a leap, there were a dozen churches in Oregon and California. There were none in the South.

This pattern was much the same for the Lutheran denomination, with the exception that there were some churches in the southern states. This was also true of the Episcopal, Methodist, Baptist, and Presbyterian groups. The Friends, Reformed, and Moravian sects followed the pattern of the Congregational churches, without, however, reaching the Far West. The Catholic Church in 1776 had its churches located chiefly around Maryland, Delaware, New Jersey, and Pennsylvania; by 1860 they had extended across the United States but were not dispersed through the Rocky Mountain states. (The only graph of this expansion is in the *Atlas of the Historical Geography of the United States,* by Paullin and Wright, published by the Carnegie Institution of Washington and the American Geographical Society of New York.)

In the next thirty years there was tremendous growth, so that by 1890 all of the larger denominations had spanned the country.

Church building lagged a little behind population growth. This lack served to introduce several uniquely American religious mission instruments. One of these was the circuit rider, who traveled far and wide serving many communities within radius of his home base. His work in a community was finished as soon as its congregation became numerically strong

Holy Name of Mary Church, Sault Ste. Marie, Michigan
(Beauchamp's Studio)

enough to put up a church building and support a minister.

Another innovation was the "arbor church," the popular expedient used in the plain states between 1855 and 1900. This was the church of revivals and camp meetings, meetings which took place in the open, in "God's first temple," under the skies and among the trees. Some of these open-air "churches" became, in a sense, invisible structures which were used again and again by either the same or different missionary groups. In the *Nebraska Advertiser* of September 5, 1861, it was reported that "a Methodist meeting has been in progress for a week in a grove of trees between Brownville and Peru," and that the attendance was large. The first such meeting held in Nebraska territory was "at John Carroll's grove in the Morris settlement in Cass County."

The so-called mission years, that period of extensive church expansion, were 1800 through 1861. Rapid as it was, this activity might have been accelerated but for one great drawback. This was the lack of trained ministers and priests. It was not until the academies and colleges could introduce training facilities that this deficiency was met at all. Many Catholic bishops established their first seminaries in their episcopal residences, beginning with a nucleus of foreign students and priests. The demand for vocations among the native-born could not be met—there was too much work of a corporeal nature to be done in a new country—and all religious training suffered a setback at the time of the Civil War enlistments and conscriptions. Often the methods of circuit rider and arbor church were combined and put into practice by a community church.

In the balance of this chapter we will look at a few of the churches of the mission years which succeeded and survived, some as the forerunners of the swing across the country.

One of these successful early missions established the Church of the Holy Family in Cahokia (now in the State of Illinois) in 1699. This Catholic church was founded by sanction of Bishop St. Vallier at Quebec in 1698 (since Illinois territory was until 1717 a dependency of Canada). The mission was French, and was under the leadership of Father François Jolliet de Montigny.

The Tamaroa Indians received the missionaries at their long journey's end; they had traveled via the Great Lakes and the Illinois and Mississippi Rivers. Within a year, the French had achieved their goal. The Mission of the Holy Family was established, and Cahokia became the first permanent white settlement along the Mississippi.

The original church was destroyed by fire, but in 1799 a new walnut log church was ready. It was built on hand-hewn timbers set upright, and the eaves were in the flaring style of Quebec. The present church is the oldest survival of French pioneer architecture from Canada to the Gulf of Mexico. Later in the nineteenth century this log and stone construction was covered with siding to protect it from the weather, and the church is now in a further process of restoration.

One of our country's smaller denominations exemplifies in fine manner the colonial approach to building and direct westward expansion. This is the Moravian Church in America, of the Northern Province. All of the original churches are still in use. "The Old Chapel" at Bethlehem, Pennsylvania, built in 1751, was the first church erected by Moravians in America. In colonial days Benjamin Franklin and George Washington worshiped here. It is of random ashlar stone construction in colonial style, sturdily built. The second church is Central Moravian Church, also at Bethlehem. This was built in 1803 and has become the "Home Congregation" of the Northern Province. This building is a fine example of colonial architecture. It was built to accommodate the expanding membership in its own vicinity, before the westward movement began.

While other churches of the Moravian group were built during this "mission period," we will span the intervening years and swing over to the Midwest, where we find a church erected in 1851 at Green Bay, Wisconsin. Green Bay East Moravian Church has an attractive tower, is built of wood, the plentiful material of the day, and shows the carry-over of the colonial pattern of architecture with the inevitable modifications of time and location.

Entry of religion into the Midwest was made early in the seventeenth century, for the waters of the St. Lawrence and the Great Lakes afforded a natural route. When France opened up this northern route and the lands it made accessible, the early explorers fostered missionary activity among the many tribes. First the Recollect Fathers were called upon, and then the Jesuits.

It was in this way that churches first came to the area of Michigan. In 1641 the Jesuits landed at the eastern tip of the Upper Peninsula at what is now the city of Sault Ste. Marie. Fathers Isaac Jogues and Raynbault were the first to arrive, Father Jogues celebrating the first Mass. These early visitations were fruitful, and from 1668 to 1696, within the protective walls of a fort and stockade, the missionary work continued. One of the youngest Jesuits assisting and exploring from this center was Father Jacques Marquette.

The work of the missionaries among the Indians was hampered for a century and more by the influence of warring colonial elements in the New World, the American Revolution, and the settling of state boundaries. But when boatloads of settlers began to arrive at Sault Ste. Marie in 1834, the first permanent church was built. Economic progress could now begin in earnest: new resources were developed, such as cop-

Beecher Bible and Rifle Church, Wabaunsee, Kansas

per and lumber and limestone, and the great schooners began to carry these materials over the waterways. There was lumber for new buildings. And the famous Father Frederic Baraga was consecrated "Bishop of the Sault."

The missionaries were now concerned with the growing communities of settlers as well as with the many tribes of Indians. To the latter task, the bishop brought great talent and a will to labor. He wrote shortly before his consecration in 1853 his masterly philological works, an invaluable grammar and a dictionary of the Otchipwe language—works not surpassed, if equaled, by any similar attempt in philological science to master a hitherto uncultivated language of savages. The bishop then turned to the matter of the settlers, and worked to establish churches and schools and missions. He has left a record of most extraordinary achievement as a pioneer of Christianity.

The present church at the Sault was built in 1881, a substantial brick structure suitable for this rugged country of severe winters. The Holy Name of Mary Church is still active, and is proclaimed one of the most beautiful old buildings in the north country.

In 1796 the Treaty of Paris brought the territory of Michigan under American rule, and in 1837 it became a State of the Union. Both the Baptists and the Catholics moved into the western part of Lower Michigan. The Catholics established a lasting mission at the Rapids of the Grand River, and the Baptists, under the ministry of the Reverend Isaac McCoy, set up a school and mission on the site which in 1824 became the city of Grand Rapids. In 1836, the Baptist school and mission closed.

It was the work of the future bishop, Father Frederic Baraga, called the "Apostle of the Chippewas," who came to the Indian villages of the Grand River, that established the

Catholic mission community. With the aid of money from the Leopoldine Mission Society of Vienna, in 1833 he set up a mission among the Indians, who were eager to have a "blackrobe" among them. From this work arose the first church, St. Andrew's, in 1849, built of "river limestone." It was built of limestone rather than wood because the river water was low and the rock could be readily quarried. This church had been preceded by the Campan church, built in 1837 and later sold to a Congregationalist group.

The present St. Andrew's, rebuilt in 1903, is a Gothic structure. It is the cathedral church of the Catholic diocese of Grand Rapids.

Two aspects of church expansion into the Midwest are exemplified by the First Presbyterian Church of Springfield, Illinois. First, while a good number of the settlers had come northward from Kentucky, there were many others who had come west, stimulated by church and missionary journals which encouraged new immigrants to direct themselves to the "Golden West." Secondly, the church's ministry was "eastern trained."

The Reverend John M. Ellis, New Hampshire-born and trained at Dartmouth and Andover Theological Seminary, came to central Illinois in 1825. He was sent by the United Domestic Missionary Society of New York. In 1828 he founded the First Presbyterian Church of Springfield, and took the first steps toward the organization of Illinois College.

The Reverend Ellis' successor, also from the East, New Jersey, achieved construction of the first church building, partly with funds obtained from an appeal in "The Home Missionary." The brick building was dedicated in 1830 and replaced thirteen years later by a larger structure.

It is of interest to point out that, aside from the "splinter" churches that were formed from this foundation, it brought to the area a consciousness of the need for education. In the first thirty-seven years of their work in Illinois, seven colleges were founded by the Presbyterians. Many were the offspring of mission activities radiating from the center point in Springfield.

Historically, the First Presbyterian Church, again through association with a historic person, is notable. From 1850 until he left Springfield in 1861, Abraham Lincoln and his family were members of the congregation. They rented pew 20 at an annual fee of thirty-six dollars. The Lincoln pew is preserved today as a memorial in the old church building; the present church was acquired in 1871. Several stained-glass windows of the present church, while all are notable, reflect the missionary activities of the followers, Sheldon Jackson and David Brainerd among others.

Between the years 1628 and 1638, three Congregational colonies were established in the East by Puritans who had emigrated from England to found a faith of their own conviction.

In the mid-nineteenth century, the New Haven colony determined to move westward to Kansas. Their mission was twofold: to establish a Congregational church there, and to promote the settlement of Kansas by an anti-slavery element.

In preparation for the trip, one hundred prospective members of the westward-bound group held meetings in the First Church of New Haven. Their problem was that, while they had sufficient funds to travel and maintain themselves on the prairie until crops could be produced, they did not have the money for weapons "to protect themselves." The Reverend Henry Ward Beecher, then pastor of Plymouth Church in Brooklyn, New York, happened to attend one of these meetings and subscribed so heartily to the plan under way

St. Paul's Episcopal Church, Tombstone, Arizona
(photo by "Frashers," Pomona, California)

that he pledged to supply whatever was necessary to send the colony on its way. Within a week of his return to Brooklyn he raised enough money to send $625 and a Bible and hymn book for every member of the colony to take to Kansas. The money raised at New Haven was enough to provide a Sharp's rifle or carbine, then the most effective small arm known in this country, for each member of the group.

This was the sendoff for the famous "Beecher Bible and Rifle Church," founded at Wabaunsee, Kansas, in 1856. At first, church services for the group were held in a grove of trees, then in a tent, then in a temporary church. During the border difficulties in Kansas, rifles were shipped free to state settlers in boxes labeled "Bibles." Pro-slavery advocates in Missouri passed by such boxes when they searched wagons and steamboats hauling freight for the new settlers. Thus the name "Beecher Bibles" was given generally to the Sharp rifles which came into Kansas during territory days.

In 1862 a stone church was constructed which still exists. The sanctuary was built of native stone, quarried in the Blue Stem hills by the parishioners and hauled to the site. All building was done by the parishioners. The woodwork was all native wood, sawed in a sawmill brought from New England to provide the colonists with lumber for their own homes.

This was a quite typical American mission enterprise because it arose in the East, and moved West with the colony, spreading the faith and exemplifying the ideal of religious freedom which, in turn, added to the social and governmental growth of the country. The church is a historic landmark; the town has not grown to its full promise, but here a mission served and a church remains.

With the crunch of wheels on the prairie, the crack of the bullmaster's whip, the creak of saddle leather, and the lurch of the stagecoach, the movement was westward. Indians, rifles, and six-guns were part of the changing scene, as was the avaricious pioneer whose only goal was exploitation of the material riches to be discovered, or plundered. There was a need for churches. These came, quietly taking their place among the elements of good, and of evil. The women prayed, and the men cursed, but the prayer prevailed. Many of the churches stand today even in the ghost towns.

St. Paul's Episcopal Church in Tombstone, Arizona, is one of these. When silver was found in the vicinity in the 1850's, a small camp of eager, and desperate, souls was set up and, with a momentary glance at eternal verities, called itself "Tombstone." There came a great crush of miners from Nevada, California, and the East, and the town grew to a metropolis of fourteen thousand.

Tombstone gained a quicksilver reputation as the wildest mining camp in the West. But there were some among the new settlers who gave a second thought to the name of the town, and, perhaps pausing to think of the transitoriness of life, began to hold religious services, first in a storeroom, then in the old courthouse. Funds were raised for a church, but a disastrous fire destroyed the bank and the money along with other buildings. A new fund was started before the ashes had cooled.

In 1882 the Reverend Endicott Peabody arrived from the East to take charge of the religious community. He was young but knowledgeable, the same man who was to become the celebrated head of Groton school in Massachusetts, hand a diploma to Franklin D. Roosevelt, and later, to officiate at his marriage to Eleanor Roosevelt.

On the Reverend Mr. Peabody's arrival in Tombstone, his first task was to erect a suitable church. Lumber was expensive and scarce, so St. Paul's was built of adobe bricks like the earlier missions. The necessary lumber for beams was hauled by oxen from the Chirachua mountains; the pews, baptismal font and reading desk were carved of black walnut. And, as a touch to demonstrate the free flow of silver, stained glass and chandeliers of the best quality were brought from the eastern seaboard.

The church became a symbol of Christianity among turbulence. Local comment upon its erection was that "Bloody Tombstone could plant a rosebush and build a church." It was a proud accomplishment. It had a quieting effect; it brought dignity to, and came to be a part of, western life. Here the famous peace officer Wyatt Earp attended services, and here are the records of the baptism of the first white child born in nearby Bisbee. And here, fifty-nine years later, Dr. Peabody returned to find the church much as it had been when he was its rector. So it stands today, the oldest Protestant church in Arizona, in a silence that endures while the six-guns rest.

Where there was gold and silver there were men, and where men went the churches went, with their mission of laying up the greatest treasure of all. The great Comstock strike turned Virginia City, Nevada, into a brawling, quick-rich town. And there in 1860 the Catholic Father Hugh Gallagher—appointed to succeed his brother, Reverend Joseph Gallagher, who had celebrated the first Mass in the town in 1858—came and built St. Mary's in the Mountains. It was the first church of any denomination in the city.

The church's life was short, for a severe storm in the winter of 1861 blew it down. A new pastor, Father Manogue, arrived and built anew in 1862, only to find that the church was too small for the growing city. A third, larger, church was built of brick at what was then the great cost of sixty-five thousand dollars, and this was considered to be "both an ornament to the city and a credit to the Catholics."

This third church saw only seven years' service, for a great

*St. Paul's Episcopal Church, Tombstone, Arizona
(photo by "Frashers," Pomona, California)*

fire swept the city in 1875. Most of the buildings were destroyed. As the fire roared and threatened to spread, Father Manogue gave his permission to dynamite the church in an effort to save part of the town. He stood and watched St. Mary's spire rise, then fall into the chaos.

The sad loss was quickly made up by subscription of the local citizens, and the fourth church was built in 1877. It was a Gothic structure, considered to have the finest interior finish of any church in the West. Its list of subscribers gives evidence of the bonanza days and the zeal of people of all classes for the dignity of public worship.

The bell of the new church was donated by a Mr. Lynch who took silver from the Comstock, sent it back east for refining, and had the bell cast. And here in this church can be seen vestments with threads of gold from the local mines woven into the fabric by European nuns. Local gold and silver were cast into the chalices and monstrance. And because the gifts of nature were rich, even further use was made of the mined wealth. Three fine paintings were bought which still hang on the walls above the altars.

This fine Gothic church succeeded in taking its place among rough and generous men. The times have changed, but the church remains in use, along with the schools and hospital.

Once the explorers had opened a path to the West, homesteaders moved in. The nineteenth century saw the fast, if painful, growth of railroads across the country, facilitating the westward migrations. When settlers arrived in Montana about mid-century, they found Indian missions already established by the Jesuit, Pierre-Jean de Smet. One of these was St. Mary's Mission at Stevensville, Montana, dating to 1841. Early relics of this mission can still be seen in a church, built

*St. Mary's in the Mountains, Virginia City, Nevada
(photo by "Frashers," Pomona, California)*

in 1866, which endures as a memorial of Father de Smet's work among the Flathead Indians.

Also in Montana is St. Ignatius Mission, which de Smet founded in 1844. The Mission is still in use, although its weathered school building has been closed for many years.

Near Tabor, South Dakota, the Bon Homme Congregational Church stands, although the once-thriving town which built it has disappeared. The church, built in 1870, is still in use, and is presently a state historic site. In back of the church is the replica of the first school in the state, a crude structure, but one that symbolizes, as does the church itself, the major forces in the shaping of the state.

Colorado's oldest Methodist church, St. James', is still in existence and still in use in Central City. This church was organized in 1859, and the present building completed in 1872. Outside its missionary function, it has a tradition as a rugged memorial in random brick and stone. The pipe organ was installed in 1899, and operated by water power until 1933, when it was converted to electricity. Its coal-burning furnace has been in use since 1897. And even the present carpet has withstood fifty-seven years of hard use!

In Colorado we come full circle in our mission excursion, for here the Spanish Catholics, followers of the early mission founders of the South and Southwest, put up an American mission. It was their last in the years classified as missionary, but it was put up on American soil. The settlers had come from the South on horseback, in covered wagons, mule trains, and on foot to seek freedom of worship. This land had first been claimed by Spain, then, after winning independence from Mexico, Texas claimed the San Luis valley and other lands in the panhandle.

But in 1854, six years after the United States had acquired clear title to this area, the settlers were busy in southwestern

St. Mary's in the Mountains, Virginia City, Nevada
(photo by "Frashers," Pomona, California)

Colorado erecting a permanent town. The first permanent church building in the present State of Colorado was erected by the Spanish in a place they named Conejos. It was built in 1855 on the left bank of the Conejos River and named "Our Lady of Guadalupe." In more than name it demonstrated the Spanish and Mexican influence, for it was constructed of adobe walls in the Spanish mission pattern, and with the typical characteristics of a fortress.

In 1926 the church was destroyed by fire, only the towers and facade remaining, but in 1948 it was rebuilt and enlarged to its present form.

III

SOME FIRST CHURCHES

The United States, having been founded in part on the principle of religious freedom and dedicated to the continuance of that principle, has thrived and benefited by the integrity of the religious-minded. Once this guarantee was achieved and the chains of persecution struck away, there was a continuous seeking of expression, and the works of Americans have and continue to be reflected in ever-increasing devotion to God. The United States of America, as no other country, should be a land of devotion, a land of churches.

There have, regrettably, been factional clashes and persecutions which seemed to deny the principle of liberty. Some have caused outbursts of violence, as when the Nativists, irked by the immigration of other freedom-seekers and incited by the Reverend Lyman Beecher, burned an Ursuline Sisters' convent at Charleston, Massachusetts; and when Philadelphia rioters in 1844 burned two Catholic churches. The mid-nineteenth century flare of bigotry rose with the Know-Nothing and "American Protective Association" movements; anti-semitism movements have been largely anti-Judaism. These acts of bigotry—properly called "little-try"—have fortunately not prevailed.

We cannot, of course, pride ourselves on having achieved perfect understanding even today. But it is a goal we must pursue, and eventually attain.

Some notable "firsts" have found a place in our historic pattern of religious striving. American freedom has also given rise to churches of "new" religions, too numerous for us to present them all.

The Lutheran Church in America had its beginning in 1664 in New York City with the erection of the "mother-church" of St. Matthew's, although for sixteen years before there had been a congregation. From this nucleus grew numerous churches which spread west and south in the manner of an opening fan.

Large numbers of German Lutheran immigrants came to America during the missionary years seeking religious free-dom from governmental dominance under King Frederick William II. One of these groups came to Wisconsin in October, 1839, arriving at Milwaukee. About half of the families remained here, but the others went twenty miles north to found Freistadt, which thus became the oldest Lutheran parish in Wisconsin. The parish is still in existence in what is now the village of Thiensville. The present church building, fourth in the parish, was erected in 1884. Hailed as the outstanding urban Lutheran church of the United States, this church epitomizes more than the continuation of religion in a new land.

Trinity Evangelical Lutheran Church has also promoted the building of schools, trained teachers, and made generous contributions to the work of missions. In many respects it is notable for having fostered music through choirs and bands,

First Church in Boston, Boston, Massachusetts
(photo by Hansen-Cambridge)

and in American civic tradition it has been the source of a rich Germanic culture which still survives in the nearby communities.

Standing at the corner of Berkeley and Marlborough Streets in Boston, Massachusetts, is the First Church in Boston, a Unitarian church founded in 1630 by John Winthrop and his followers, who set down the covenant which begins: "Wee whose names are hereunder written, being by his most wise & good Providence brought together into this part of America in the Bay of Massachusetts, & desirous to unite our selves into one Congregation, or Church, under the Lord Jesus Christ our Head, in such sort as becometh all those whom He hath Redeemed, & Sanctyfied to Himselfe . . ."

The first church was erected in 1632; the second, seven years later, was destroyed by fire; and the third, known as "Old Brick" for many years, was built in 1713. The fourth Meeting House was put up in 1808, the fifth and present church in 1867.

Constructed of Roxbury pudding-stone, designed by Ware and Van Brunt, the church is in simplified Gothic style, dim and quiet within, with shadows interestingly cast by the massive hammer beams. The most impressive aspects of this church are associated with the lives of notable men who have served and worshiped here. On the walls are memorials and tablets commemorating, among others, President John Quincy Adams, Robert Treat Paine, Benjamin Wadsworth, president of Harvard College, and Ralph Waldo Emerson.

The First Church's Communion Silver is very old and rare, some of it dating from before the founding of the church. This silver is on exhibition at the Museum of Fine Arts, Boston, but is available for use at the church whenever needed. Among this collection is the Governor John Winthrop Cup which bears the London date letter 1610.

John Winthrop Cup (First Church in Boston)

Built on disputed territory, which was claimed by Massachusetts, Connecticut, and Rhode Island, the Seventh-Day Baptists' Meeting-house was erected on the bank of the Pawcatuck River in 1680. It was largely through the tenacious efforts of the early settlers that the Misquamicut area became a part of the Commonwealth of Rhode Island. The church was formed by a group of members of the Newport Church. In 1708 a charter was granted by the State of Rhode Island, and the church was thereafter known as the First Seventh-day Baptist Church of Hopkinton, located at what now is known as Ashaway, Rhode Island.

A second church, replacing the old meeting-house with its stove in the center of the hall, was erected in 1835 on the site of the first church. It was moved to Ashaway in 1852 and enlarged to its present form in 1882.

This first church and its members played a decisive part in matters of the denomination's organization in America, in the evolution of Rhode Island as a state, and in the struggle for civil and religious liberty. Directly from this beginning more than fifteen churches have sprung, and attributable to it also is the founding of Brown University and other schools. It is revered as the mother-church of the denomination.

By 1785, the Catholics of New York were able to look back on the period of political disenfranchisement which had followed the Colony enactment of 1711, and on June 16 of that year an act of incorporation of Catholic property was secured through the aid of the Spanish Royal Minister. This led to the immediate purchase of farmland on what is now Barclay Street. The purchase was made from the Trinity Church Society of the Protestant Episcopal Church of New York, and this land became the site of St. Peter's, the first Catholic Church erected in New York City after the establishment of the Federal Constitution.

The cornerstone of St. Peter's was laid on October 5, 1785, and the church opened for services thirteen months later. The oldest Roman Catholic church building in Manhattan, it was remodeled in 1838. On the pediment above the six tall columns of its entrance stands a statue of St. Peter holding the keys of heaven and hell. St. Patrick's Cathedral was later to be built on land owned by St. Peter's Corporation.

The old stone church of Norriton, near Fairview Village, Pennsylvania, was the first of many Presbyterian churches (there are now some twelve thousand) built in the United States. The meeting house built in 1698 by white settlers, undoubtedly Holland-Dutch by nationality, replaced a log structure dating to 1678.

The old Norriton building was used as a hospital after the battle of Germantown in the American Revolution. Here George Washington visited the wounded, and here Benjamin Franklin and David Rittenhouse worshiped. From this church and its small congregation came a chaplain, the Reverend Daniel McCalla, thirteen officers, and eighteen men, all soldiers of the Revolution.

The old building, battered in the wars and ravaged by time, has remained. In 1940 the high pulpit and pews, in the best style of the Colonial period, were set in place, refurbishing the church interior and supplanting the antique pieces which had been torn out in 1844. Now only an annual service is held there, but the Lower Providence Church of Norriton has given rise to a wide heritage. This is evident in its daughter-churches: Old Pine Church of Philadelphia; Rehoboth Church of Rehoboth, Maryland; and East Liberty Church of Pittsburgh.

The old Cane Ridge Meeting-house, built in 1791, has unique distinction and significance for the followers of the Christian Church (Disciples of Christ). The log-constructed church is preserved as a memorial, and is now enclosed, for protection, within a modern building. The denomination says of this church: "It is overlaid with all manner of sacred associations, which, taken together, make it the oldest and most unique shrine among us. It was here in 1804 that Barton W. Stone, its minister, first proclaimed the cardinal principles that gave birth to the Christian Church or the Disciples of Christ."

The building was erected in what is now Bourbon County, Kentucky, in the year before Kentucky entered the Union as a state. The builders were settlers who had migrated from North Carolina under the leadership of a Presbyterian minister, the Reverend Robert W. Finley. They had been directed to this vicinity by Daniel Boone, who himself had called this section "The Cane Ridge" because of the extensive cane brakes found there.

The church was built of blue ash logs. It has a "boxed up" pulpit, approached by several steps. Three immense girders, sixteen inches square, hewn with a broadax, tied the walls together at the ceiling. The sheathing was sawed by a whip-saw, and the roof of clapboards was attached to this sheathing and held in place by wooden pins. The old church had a gallery where the slaves sat, entrance to which was gained by means of a ladder. The floor was originally earth, but at an early date a puncheon floor was laid. While modernized somewhat over the years, this remains as one of the earliest Protestant churches of the western settlements.

The place of the first Catholic parish in the continental United States is marked by the Cathedral of St. Augustine at St. Augustine, Florida. While the Cathedral was built in 1791–1797, its parish records date from 1597. The church of Spanish design stands overlooking the Plaza de la Constitución, a landmark of the country's earliest history, referred to as the "Birthplace of the Nation."

It was a Spaniard, Juan Ponce de Leon, a colleague of

St. Peter's Church, Barclay Street, New York City

Christoper Columbus, who, in search of the "Fountain of Youth," landed in the area of St. Augustine in 1513 and by so doing won the region for the King of Spain. It was a second Spaniard, Pedro Menéndez de Avilés, who came to crush a Huguenot settlement and stayed to found our country's first city at St. Augustine in 1565, and a Spanish missionary, Francisco López de Mendoza Grajales, who built the country's first mission. On this start followed the vast immigration from Europe, Asia, and Africa which eventually raised the United States to a position of world power.

Spain lost her Florida holdings to England in 1763, and regained the territory by the Treaty of Paris twenty years later. In 1784 the King of Spain sent two Irish priests to Florida. The first of these was Reverend Thomas Hassett, known as the founder of America's first free school. The second priest, Father Michael O'Reilly, was the builder of the Cathedral in this historic city.

The cornerstone was laid in 1791, funds having been raised from property owned by the St. Augustine Church in Havana, Cuba, and from parishioners. Part of the material was salvaged from the ruined shrines of Tolemato, an Indian mission outside the city, and Nuestra Señora de la Leche, which had been destroyed by the British. The Cathedral is Spanish in design, the belfry is distinctly Moorish. The coquina rock of which the church is built was quarried from Anastasia Island across the river from the city. The stones were cut by hand and ferried to the building site on barges. Much of the original building remains, although it was partially damaged by fire in 1887. Some claim that the heat of this fire fused the soft coquina rock walls into their present granite hardness.

As the bells of the old belfry were stilled by the fire, a campanile was erected during the renovation, equipped with a chime of bells and a clock. Below the clock is the sun dial, originally on the church façade, on which a Latin inscription

Old Pine Church, Philadelphia, Pennsylvania
(Presbyterian Historical Society)

reads: "The hours perish and we must account for them." Twelve stained glass windows tell the story of the parish patron, Saint Augustine, after his conversion from paganism. The altars, of fine Carrara marble, follow Renaissance models, while the Stations of the Cross on the Cathedral walls are styled after Overbeck originals in the Pauline Chapel of the Vatican in Rome.

This oldest parish has since its founding seen every nationality of the world represented there. The records of the parish "reveal more than the activities of one church; they tell the complete story of the United States of America in the yellowed pages of four centuries."

Maryland's first Catholic church is that of St. Ignatius, which stands at St. Inigoes. This was the first Catholic mission established in British North America and it is the oldest Catholic foundation with permanent existence and activity within the limits of the original thirteen colonies. It is certainly the most ancient Jesuit establishment in the United States, and probably the oldest in the world that has been in continuous possession of the Society of Jesus.

Its history as a church is coeval with the settlement of Maryland. It was located within a mile of the spot where the Jesuit, Father Andrew White, the pioneer missioner of Maryland, raised the cross a few hours after the second Lord Baltimore's vessels, the *Ark* and the *Dove,* had arrived from England and landed their passenger pilgrims in St. Mary's city in 1634. From this center, Andrew White, first historian of Maryland and literary patriarch, set forth on his apostleship along the Potomac River to Piscatawny, Port Tobacco, and Anacostia. St. Ignatius' three hundred-odd years tell a colorful story of the padlocking of the church by royal order; the kidnaping of its priest and his return to England on a commandeered Dutch vessel; the tearing down of the church by its people, and their transporting its bricks five miles down-

Rehoboth Presbyterian Church, Rehoboth, Maryland
(Presbyterian Historical Society)

river by barge; the relocation of the building by the water-side. The story includes bombardment by British cannon and raids by British soldiers and American Indians.

The first brick church, replacing an Indian hut that had belonged to a Yaccomoco chief and served as a crude chapel, was erected in 1636. It is referred to as the "New Chapel at St. Maries" in one of the first land-patents on record, that of Cuthbert Fenwick in 1641.

In 1704 Governor Seymour, presiding at the meeting of the council at St. Mary's city, heard complaint brought against Fathers Brooke and Hunter for violation of the so-called "law of 1700" which made the liturgy of the Church of England and the use of the Book of Common Prayer obligatory in every church or other place of worship. The defendants were refused their request of counsel, and the chronicles of colonial Maryland tell us that since it was "the first offense," the governor was instructed to reprimand the offenders; this he did in language (according to the chronicle) "which was singularly conspicuous for its arrogant and intolerant spirit." Thereupon the members of the council decided that, "Such use of the popish Chapel of the City of St. Mary's County where there is a protestant church . . . is both scandalous and offensive to the government."

Governor Seymour in 1704 issued an order directing the sheriff of the county to lock up the "popish chapel in the city of St. Mary's and to keep the key thereof," and "that no person presume to make use thereof under any pretense whatever." Now mute and padlocked, the church was demolished and its bricks transported five miles south by its displaced parishioners. There in 1705 a manor house was built, in the privacy of which the people of the parish worshiped God in peace for forty years.

The manor's importance began to decline when a new and fairly large church, built a half-mile away, completely sup-

Cane Ridge Meeting-house, Paris, Kentucky
(Cane Ridge Preservation Project)

planted it as a place of worship. The chapel built behind the manor in 1745 had proved too small, so in 1784 construction was begun on a larger St. Ignatius church. This was a quaint brick church with box pews, servants' gallery, and "Amen" corner. During its construction Negroes tended the fires in which bricks were baked all night. During their watch, the Negroes kept themselves awake strumming banjos, singing old southern songs, and eating the midnight meal sent out to them by their families. The church completed in 1788 is still standing, though it is no longer the center of the parish nor a place of regular worship—only a memorial of the past.

Americans can take courage from the history of this church and its people. Its history renders incarnate the ideal of religious freedom for which the pilgrims searched and suffered—an ideal which our founding Fathers framed in the Constitution under which our Republic lives, an ideal which makes America today the object of hope for those longing for the peace of the world.

With a figurative cross-country leap, we come to San Francisco where, if not the first church of the denomination in the country, the first in the Far West was established.

The First Unitarian Society of San Francisco was founded in the wild, rough days of the gold rush, on October 21, 1850. The Reverend Charles Andrews Farley was the minister, but he was only on the West coast temporarily. The congregation erected its first building in 1853, the second in 1864, and the third, and present, one in 1889. This building was restored in 1906. At the time of the dedication of the second building, the poet John Greenleaf Whittier wrote a hymn for the occasion.

Perhaps the most colorful years of the church were those of the ministry of the Reverend Thomas Starr King. He had come west in 1860 expecting to stay only a year, but then the

Cane Ridge Meeting-house, Paris, Kentucky
(Cane Ridge Preservation Project)

Civil War began and it became a matter of national concern that California be saved for the Union. There were mixed sentiments in California, some powerful men favoring the cause of the Confederacy. Starr King readily undertook a new "calling" when the realization of the position of California in the cause of the Federal Government came to him. It was largely because of his efforts in preaching and lecturing throughout the state that California was saved for the Union cause.

To this task Starr King added another. By his lectures in the mining camps he raised one-and-a-half million dollars for the Sanitary Commission, which was later to become the American Red Cross. The funds were used for the care of sick and wounded soldiers of the Civil War. For these and other works of civic importance, Starr King is one of the two Californians honored in the National Capitol's Hall of Fame.

When the present church was being dedicated, a gift of a marble baptismal font was made to the congregation by the Reverend Henry W. Bellows, pastor of the First Congregational Church in New York and president of the Sanitary Commission. Also in recognition of Starr King's work, the same gentleman presented a rare and valuable Bible to the church. And its own congregation raised the funds to install in this present church one of the finest pipe organs in the West.

The marble tomb of Thomas Starr King is located in the front of the church he had come to assist "for a year."

An American "first" church in the literal sense of the word is the First Church of Christ, Scientist, at Boston. It was organized by Mary Baker Eddy, discoverer and founder of Christian Science, in 1892, and is the culmination of a long-cherished hope. The first building in which Christian Science services were held was perhaps a small frame church build-

First Unitarian Church, San Francisco, California
(photo by H. Blair)

ing in Oconto, Wisconsin, but by 1892 Mrs. Eddy's following had grown so large that she urged the Church Directors to erect an outstanding building which would be looked upon as "The Mother Church."

The services of several eminent Boston architects were solicited, and they submitted designs. Funds were raised slowly but courageously by the founder and directors, and the work began on October 19, 1893. In May of the following year the cornerstone was laid, and on the wall was placed this inscription: "The First Church of Christ, Scientist, erected Anno Domini, 1894. A testimonial to our beloved teacher, the Reverend Mary Baker Eddy: Discoverer and Founder of Christian Science; author of its text-book, Science and Health with Key to the Scriptures; President of the Massachusetts Metaphysical College, and the first Pastor of this Denomination."

The church was further decorated with stained glass windows of religious significance. Of Romanesque architecture, adapted, the church held its first service on January 6, 1895. It is the headquarters of the Christian Science movement, and a Boston landmark.

In 1904 work was begun on the Extension, contiguous to the original Mother Church, which was made necessary by increased membership. The problem of adapting the available property, which was shaped somewhat like an hourglass, was thought insurmountable. Yet the plans went forward and the church was completed in 1906, the largest church building in the city of Boston. In the message of the Founder read at the dedication of the Extension is a tribute to the edifice: "a magnificent temple wherein to enter and pray."

First Church of Christ, Scientist, Boston, Massachusetts

IV

CHURCHES ACROSS THE COUNTRY

Churches, like people, may win distinction in a variety of ways. It goes without saying that every church is a unique achievement. Every church stands not only as a structure erected to house a community's religious activity, but as a symbol of every man's search for his ultimate goal. Our hundreds of thousands of churches must be reckoned in any evaluation of our country's intrinsic worth, and as our material wealth increases, our churches increase yearly in number and membership.

In this chapter we will attempt, by leaps and bounds, to cover the country, East to West, North to South. A random sampling is all we can manage, since there is scarcely a hamlet, town, or city in every state which doesn't have a church of historic importance. But we will look only at some of those which have a claim to fame by virtue of their architectural beauty, association with a page of history, or contribution to our country's civic scene.

In Boston there is one edifice that illustrates well our concept of the kind of social role played by religion in America. The present Temple Adath Israel, a synagogue built in 1907, stands at Langwood Avenue and Plymouth Street in that city; it has been described as having been "built after the style of Solomon's Temple." Temple Israel was the outgrowth of a first temple, Ohabei Shalom, which was founded by the Jewish community in 1842.

Twelve years later a forward-looking group founded and built the first Temple Adath Israel, in 1854. As Arthur Mann says in *Growth and achievement: Temple Israel, 1854–1954,* it was "founded when Boston led the way in the New England Renaissance. The period was characterized by growth, experimentation, and discovery, by the creation of a liberal literature, liberal religions, and liberal institutions. It was foremost a period of democratic aspiration in which reformers succeeded in extending rights and privileges to disadvantaged groups. Contemporaries called it the 'age of newness,' for they were less concerned to obey than to transcend the past."

From this Temple, operating and serving in a community of heralded religious freedom which became actual, sprang numerous social benefits. The Hebrew Sheltering Home; the Hebrew Industrial School, the precursor of the Hecht Neighborhood House; "Country Camp" for girls and women; the Hebrew Free Burial Society and the Free Employment Bureau; the first Federation of Jewish Charities, are but a few of the contributions made to our society.

In New York City there is a church of both historic and

social importance which at one time acquired an interesting appellation that has clung through the years. This is the Episcopal Church of the Transfiguration, known since the 1870's as "The Little Church Around the Corner."

The Church of the Transfiguration was founded on October 1, 1848, when its first service was held in the home of a layman, Lawson Carter. The church was built in 1849, on what was then the outskirts of the city, between Madison Square and Murray Hill. It was the first church to be founded in this country to carry on what was then called the "Oxford Movement" to revive the full Catholic faith in the Anglican Church.

Notable in this church's service has been the ministry of the Reverend Dr. George Hendric Houghton, the founding rector. Dr. Houghton had a span of forty-nine years of service, and has fondly been called by his followers "our first American saint." His distinction arose from a variety of works, and from his advice to everyone: "Be kind!" During the Draft Riots of 1863, he gave asylum in the rectory basement to escaped slaves while threatening mobs waited to kill the fugitives.

Perhaps the most outstanding social service performed by the church, however, was the establishment of "bread lines" to aid the unemployed and destitute. This work was originated in the post-Civil War days by Dr. Houghton and continued during the two financial crises of this century—the panic of 1907 and the great depression of the thirties. This relief work was made possible through public donations. Even today the social work of the church is continuing among the young, and the needy, of New York City.

The church, apart from its beauty of appointments, its windows, altars, and statues, is noted for its association with theatre people. Members of the theatrical profession have

Church of the Transfiguration, New York City
(photo by Lawrence D. Thornton)

adopted this church as a shrine. In fact, its more popular name was gained in 1870 when the pastor of a fashionable Madison Avenue congregation refused burial services to George Holland, an actor, and suggested to Joseph Jefferson, a friend of the deceased, that he try "the little church around the corner." The Episcopal Actors' Guild of America has headquarters in the church building.

For years the Little Church has also been known as a favorite place for marriages. It is said that more marriages are solemnized here in the Church of the Transfiguration than in any other church in the world (although marriage is refused to divorced persons), and many of the children born of these marriages are brought to the church to be baptized.

In a Foundation Day sermon, the Reverend Dr. Randolph Ray, the present Rector (regrettably to retire on June 11, 1958), said, "The Little Church, like a human character, has built its way, full of personality and reflecting beauty, until you think of it as one of the most beautiful parish churches in the country, because the stones that make its walls are so impregnated with God and humanity."

Plymouth Church of the Pilgrims in Brooklyn, N.Y., a Congregational church in organization and affiliation, is another church formed by the merging of two historic congregations, this in 1934. The Church of the Pilgrims had been founded in 1844 and Plymouth Church in 1847. Each of these congregations had had a first minister of exceptionally long tenure. The pastorate of Richard Salter Storrs at the Church of the Pilgrims lasted fifty-four years, while Henry Ward Beecher served for forty years at Plymouth Church. Both men were gifted preachers, and they have had able successors, both before and since the congregations' union.

The church property is bounded on three sides by Orange,

Plymouth Church of the Pilgrims, Brooklyn, New York

CARL A. RUDISILL LIBRARY
LENOIR RHYNE COLLEGE

Hicks, and Cranberry Streets. The extensive plant includes the sanctuary from whose pulpit Mr. Beecher "sold" a slave girl and thus raised the money to purchase her freedom. Visitors are shown a pew bearing a silver plate inscribed with a facsimile of Abraham Lincoln's signature. This is where Lincoln sat when he came to hear Beecher on the Sunday before his own famous Cooper Union address. The new Hillis Hall with adjacent chapel, and a church house which provides classrooms, administrative offices, bowling alleys, and a gymnasium for the activities of the congregation, are located on the church property.

Another New York edifice, the foremost house of worship of Reformed Judaism, stands on Fifth Avenue at Sixty-fifth Street. Congregation Emanu-El was founded in 1845 and merged with Congregation Beth-El in 1927. Temple Emanu-El was completed in 1929, and is the largest synagogue built in modern times.

The design of the Temple, with its great recessed arch on Fifth Avenue, is Romanesque in the Italian-basilica style. The Beth-El chapel is a Byzantine twin-domed structure. The main auditorium of the Temple is 77 feet wide between piers and 150 feet long; auditorium and galleries together seat twenty-five hundred worshipers. Decoration is traditional, employing such symbols as the Shield of David, which appears again and again in mosaics and windows. Flowers and fruits are also lavishly-used motifs in the designs and stained glass.

Under the Temple is the Isaac M. Wise Memorial Hall, seating fifteen hundred, which is provided with a stage, kitchen, and banquet facilities for social activities of the congregation.

Toward the south, at Alexandria, Virginia, is St. Mary's

Plymouth Church of the Pilgrims, Brooklyn, New York

Catholic Church. It began as a parish holding public worship in 1795, but before that it had functioned outside the city because of laws which banned from the state all churches except those of the Established Church. Catholic worship in Virginia was first permitted in 1785.

It was in 1776 that the State Convention adopted George Mason's Declaration of Rights, the sixteenth section of which granted "the fullest toleration in the exercise of religion according to the dictates of conscience, unpunished and unrestrained by magistrate; unless, under color of religion, any may disturb the peace, happiness or safety of society." Following this, in 1785, the "Act Establishing Religious Freedom" was passed, and the Catholic Church was permitted to preach, hold services, and erect churches.

Actually, the church began in the home of Colonel John Fitzgerald, an Irish-Catholic immigrant. Fitzgerald performed notably in the American Revolution, becoming an aide-de-camp, and a close friend, of General Washington. The first recorded death in the parish is that of an escaped indentured servant of George Washington named Cavan Boa, who died at the age of thirty-five in 1798. His is the oldest tombstone in St. Mary's cemetery.

Under William Penn's Constitution of 1701 (his last legislative act before leaving his Quaker colony to return to England) the principles of civil liberty and the unconditional equality of all religious creeds were firmly established. It was these principles which brought to Pennsylvania thousands of freedom-loving people not tolerated or encouraged elsewhere: German expatriates from a war-ravaged homeland, Mennonites, Dunkers, Moravians; Indians and Negroes escaping methodical subjugation; Scotch-Irish Presbyterians; Swedes and Welsh; and Roman Catholics of various origins.

Temple Emanu-El, New York City *(Congregation Emanu-El)*

While German Roman Catholics were a minority even in this haven of minorities, they founded a church which "was to be the first exclusively national church in the United States," Holy Trinity. German residents of Philadelphia built this church in 1789, two years after Pennsylvania became a state of the Union—one of the original thirteen.

The record of Holy Trinity is one of trials and misunderstandings—but internal ones brought on by its challenge of the bishop's authority, and the errors of "trusteeism" (lay trustees assuming the "corporate" rights of the church authorities).

Twice the church suffered damage by fire, in 1860 and 1891, twice it was rebuilt, and it is now undergoing restoration. Holy Trinity's claim to distinction is that here in 1797 was opened the first Catholic orphan asylum in the United States. A parochial school had also been opened in the church basement five years earlier. In recent years there has been a gradual change in the originally German character of the congregation. Today the church serves a steadily increasing number of Puerto Ricans.

There is an interesting anecdote connected with a church a step farther south. In Swanquarter, North Carolina, the Methodist Church was once lifted up by floodwaters, moved, and set down, undamaged, on a plot of land which the congregation had wanted but had been unable to obtain from the owner. After the flood, the owner of the land hurried down to the Register of Deeds and deeded the property to the Methodist Church without cost, saying, "I had plans for that land, but it appears God has His, too!"

Christ Church, Mobile, Alabama

THE SOUTH

The churches of the southern United States began to be founded several decades later than those of the Northeast. With the exception of the earliest mission, the pattern of mission development, mentioned in Chapter Two, followed two distinct lines: one down the East coast and then swinging west, the other a diagonal line southwestward from the Northeast to Texas. The fullest expansion of this activity took place in the first half of the nineteenth century, and was undertaken by the Episcopal, Presbyterian, Lutheran, Moravian, Methodist, Baptist, and Catholic churches.

Rather than attempt to follow the mission pattern, since the tesserae that make up the mosaic of churches in the South is varied and at first scattered, we approach the Southland from the East coast, and move westward.

During the Civil War, many churches were concerned with religion among the slaves, and with national issues. Undoubtedly because of financial losses during the war, the missionary progress of these churches was, for the time, hampered.

The first Protestant church built in Mobile, Alabama, was located just outside the west gate of Fort Charlotte, where Anglican Church services had been held by a British chaplain as early as 1760. Christ Church of Mobile was erected here in 1823. The building itself was largely the result of laymen's efforts and interest; a minister was not given charge of the church until six years later. In the interim, services were held by anyone who would tarry and preach, and lay-reading was resorted to as an alternative when necessary.

This Episcopal church also served for community social activities, and it was during a Fourth of July celebration that the floor gave way. After a period of making do in temporary quarters, the congregation saw its way clear to begin work on the present church in 1835. A large part of the building subscription was in labor, so many days' work by so many slaves, and the project took five years. The church is constructed of brick covered with plaster, and its walls are four feet thick at the base, decreasing in thickness as they rise in height. Originally this church had galleries around three sides in which slaves were seated.

Christ Church was almost destroyed in a hurricane in 1900, and, after being rebuilt, suffered a second like disaster nine years later. The repaired church has lost its steeple, but it has sturdy beauty, fashioned along classic Greek lines.

After lamentations that there was "not a house of worship among us," a small Episcopal congregation put up a "little red brick" affair in Montgomery, Alabama, in 1837. Before the construction of St. John's, its little congregation had used the Methodist and Baptist churches for their devotions. Unfortunately, *after* its construction it soon proved too small to accommodate the growing population of prosperous, busy Montgomery.

A memorable description of the Montgomery of this period once appeared in the *Advertiser:* "Montgomery just before the war, I consider, was the most interesting and pleasant city in the South. What a grand race of men and women filled and brightened the elegant and tasteful homes, adorning its level thoroughfares and picturesque eminences. They were the genuine and unadulterated outcome of a civilization to the excellence of which the history of the world can furnish no parallel. Cultured, intelligent, honest, liberal, chivalrous, independent, unselfish and refined. 'And the women,' as Steele said, 'were a liberal education!' " It would seem that so admirable a society would scarcely need a church at all, but the fact is that such a society usually recognizes keenly the value of religious activity.

A larger church was needed. St. John's congregation was forced to abandon its little red brick structure; a notable English immigrant architect, Frank Wills, was hired to design a church. He produced one of Gothic beauty, patterned after a church in Coventry, England, one of those destined for destruction in World War II. St. John's was built in lavish times; the seventeen-year period between the completion of Trinity Church in New York in 1846 and the beginning of the Civil War is the greatest era of Episcopal church building in America. In Alabama alone, from 1850 to 1860 eighteen Episcopal churches were built, the new St. John's being finished in 1854 and considered a flower among them. Around it, in the "elegant homes," the men of the Montgomery Blues and the Montgomery Rifles added glamor to the social life and lively dances of the first days of war. And it was to St. John's that the newly elected President of the Confederate States, Jefferson Davis, then fifty-three years old, drove up in a carriage in the Spring of 1861 with his wife and their three children, Maggie, young Jeff, and Joe. In the same year, the Secession Convention of Southern Churches was held in the church.

From the church of gay Montgomery, St. John's became, in the immediate post-war years, a soup-kitchen. In 1867, the army took control of the Southern states and a military constitution went into effect. St. John's survived a temporary closing under General Order No. 38, when state and church clashed over the ruling which attempted to "overturn constitutional religious freedom and to prescribe forms of worship," but lived on to inaugurate the Harvest Home Service in the 1877 depression, and to become an educational leader.

It was during this vigorous period of building that the Episcopal Church of St. Andrew's was erected at Prairieville, Alabama. It is modestly unique, one of the most picturesque churches in the South. While no longer holding regular services, this church served its purpose well during the days of slavery.

The building of St. Andrew's was completed in 1854, erected entirely by slave labor. Two Negro master carpenters, Joe Glasgow and Peter Lee, were the chief builders. Peter Lee was a quite remarkable artisan, doing by hand all the carving on both the interior and exterior of the church. The exquisite wood figures in the rail are specimens of his work. Because of the lack of wood stains and varnishes, the interior walls were painted with a substitute made up of brewed tobacco juice, and this has acted not only as a preservative but also as a coloring that survives to the present day.

St. Andrew's is one of America's most picturesque and charming churches, and its old days of service among the plantation workers are a record that will long stand.

While the Catholic Church in North America had its beginning under the Spanish in Florida, and to the northwest under the French, it was not until the "building period" of the nineteenth century that progress was made toward the southwest.

Tennessee was at that time the western part of North Carolina, and the lines of influence and eventual division of territory had not yet been defined. The territory had known the domination of the French, Spanish, and English, all of whom still made claims upon it. Via the Ohio and the Mississippi Rivers, missionaries to the area came down from the East and up from New Orleans. In the eighteenth century the territory was called Mero, after the Governor of New Orleans (who claimed territorial privileges), and it enjoyed his guarantee of religious freedom.

The first decades of the nineteenth century saw much missionary activity in the work of the Catholic Church in the area. But it was in 1844 that the first Cathedral of Nashville, Tennessee was built. It is no longer the cathedral of the diocese but is a familiar landmark of the capital city. The building was located in the heart of the town. Designed by William Strickland, the architect of the capitol building, it was hailed by him as his "finest work in ecclesiastical structures." It is of Greek Revival style and is a chaste and beautiful specimen of that architecture. It was with this classic building that Catholic religious activity in the state began on a "permanent" basis.

Going farther south, we find in Atlanta, Georgia, a Catholic church which had a stirring role in the Civil War years. The church of the Immaculate Conception was erected in 1848, a crude little frame building that was called only "the Catholic Church in Atlanta," but it did boast a painting, a beautiful copy of Murillo's "Immaculate Conception."

It was during the Civil War that the little church served most gallantly, for its pastor was Father Thomas O'Reilly, a fearless and decisive man. It so happened that, all within a rather close area had been erected the Catholic church, City Hall, the Court House, and St. Philip's Episcopal, Trinity Methodist, the Second Baptist, and Central Presbyterian churches. During the bitter siege of Atlanta in 1864, Father O'Reilly, as the only Catholic chaplain available, served the wounded of both armies, Confederate and Federal. As the war moved in closer on the city, the entire town was ordered destroyed. When Father O'Reilly, because of his ministrations to the soldiers, learned of this order, he went to General

Slocum of Sherman's Army and boldly demanded that the City Hall, Court House, and all churches in the area of the Catholic church be spared or he would compel all Catholics in the Federal forces to leave the ranks.

The bold gesture succeeded. The buildings were spared, except for the little frame Catholic church, which was shattered by shells. The rest of the city was burned. And as a bitter aftermath, the Federal troops, to justify the general's order to spare these churches, made a stable of St. Philip's, a slaughterhouse of the Presbyterian church, a storehouse of the Methodist church, and a hospital of the shelled Catholic church, where the floors were stained with the blood of the wounded. Afterward, when the people of Atlanta returned to find charred and ruined homes, they gained shelter in the church buildings, hanging burlap in the aisles as curtains, and using the pews as bunks.

It was not until 1873 that the damaged Catholic church was torn down and a new building erected. At that time, it was given the name Immaculate Conception, the title under which the Blessed Virgin is Patroness of the United States. It continued in service, becoming a leading church in parochial education, and remains today the mother-church of the state and a lasting shrine.

Begun in the first year of peace at the close of the Civil War, St. Mary's Catholic Church of Mobile, Alabama, was finished in 1867. Its history lies in the years following the Civil War, but most famous is its second pastor, Father Abram J. Ryan, priest, poet, noted orator. Father Ryan had served as a Confederate Army chaplain. His brother, a soldier in the same forces, was killed, his body unrecovered, on an unknown battlefield. Thus the priest-poet, whose famous poem "The Conquered Banner" was called the finest to come out of the Civil War, knew the bitterness of war, but could write:

> *Furl that banner, softly, slowly!*
> *Treat it gently—it is holy—*
> *For it droops above the dead.*

As pastor, Father Ryan gave civic service that is still remembered—as is the church he served which stands today in continuing memory of this priest and patriot.

In Port Gibson, Mississippi, stands the church known as "the Church with the hand pointing heavenward." The First Presbyterian Church was founded in 1807, and the present structure erected in 1859.

Perpetuated atop the spire, "The Hand" has become a widely known symbol—a reverent sign. The idea was adopted as a tribute to a beloved early minister, the Reverend Zebulon Butler, whose characteristic preaching gesture was a clenched and upraised hand. The first hand was wooden, carved by a local craftsman, and covered with gold leaf which shone in the southern sunlight. But in the 1890's the old wooden hand became so full of woodpecker holes and so weather-beaten that it was replaced by the hand of galvanized metal which tops the present spire. The size of the hand is twelve feet from the base of the wrist to the tip of the finger, the tip of the spire being 165 feet from the ground.

While this novel and unusual feature has made the church famous, First Presbyterian has to its lasting credit one hundred and fifty years of service. It was a landmark of the beautiful city in the days of slavery and during the Civil War. It was at one time lighted by the oil chandeliers from the river steamboat the *Robert E. Lee.* These chandeliers have now been electrified. This church was also the center which gave

*Church of the Immaculate Conception, Natchitoches, Louisiana
(Guillet Studio)*

rise to Chamberlain-Hunt Academy. It continues in service
—its reverent sign a tireless reminder of man's highest goal.

In the brawling coastal town of Galveston, Texas, Trinity
Episcopal Church was organized in 1841. A year after its
founding, the building was erected, set on block pilings to
raise it above the mud flats. The moving force behind its
construction was Dr. Benjamin Eaton. The present building,
Gothic and noble in appearance, was put up in 1855.

The remarkable thing about Trinity Episcopal Church is
not when it was built, but the fact that it survived to give
tremendous service in a city that was constantly changing. As
a church it passed through wars, panics, epidemics, and
hurricanes which twice damaged it. As an institution it has
given rise to civic and cultural endeavors, education, active
church societies, scouting, and a fine choir. Its history has
been prepared in great detail in an eight-hundred-page
volume.*

The Roman Catholic diocese of Natchitoches, Louisiana,
was created in 1853. Shortly thereafter, Bishop Augustus
Aloysius Marie Martin commissioned M. C. Melvin to draft
plans for a suitable cathedral, and the contract for its construction was signed on December 12, 1857. Work on the
building began in 1858, and progress continued steadily until
interrupted by the Civil War in 1861. It was not until 1892
that the structure was completed in accordance with the
original plans with the addition of the present sanctuary and
sacristies. The Cathedral was re-dedicated by Bishop Antoine
Durier at that time.

In 1910 the episcopal see was moved away from Natchi-

* W. M. Morgan, *Trinity Protestant Episcopal Church, Galveston,
Texas, 1841–1953* (Houston, The Anson Jones Press, 1954).

Church of the Immaculate Conception, Natchitoches, Louisiana
(Guillet Studio)

toches. The building, since then no longer a cathedral, was completely renovated in 1956, and the portico added at the front. The four chandeliers, imported from Italy, are strikingly beautiful with their red and white glass beads.

Bishop Martin and Very Reverend Pierre Felix Dicharry, first Vicar General of the diocese, are buried here.

THE MIDWEST

The flow of immigrants from the East coast was rapid and steady in the first half of the nineteenth century. Church groups hastily organized to meet the demand, but they could not keep pace with the great numbers arriving from Europe. The ingress was caused by many factors: the Napoleonic wars, oppression and changing political life in Germany, famine in Ireland, and the Industrial Revolution and its consequent poor social conditions in England. The Lutheran, Presbyterian, Methodist, and Catholic churches were making every effort to meet the missionary demands. All were handicapped because of the lack of trained ministers and priests.

The State of Ohio received many of the new settlers after the American Revolution and the determination of American and French claims to territory. The church movement was largely from Pennsylvania westward. As the churches spread, the architecture of the East coast moved with them and, with local variations, became the accepted form.

In the village of Tallmadge, Ohio, stands the First Congregational Church, hailed as a "perfect example of Late Colonial churches of pure Connecticut type." It is one of the finest of the state's early churches, reflecting the best features of its New England forerunners. Dedicated in 1825, it is said to be the oldest church in the state with a continuous function as a place of worship. It stands two stories high and is

College First Church of God, Findlay, Ohio   (B & J Photo Service)

surmounted by a square tower, an open, octagonal belfry, and a weathervane.

The church and the town were products of the utopian plan of one man, David Bream, to found a Congregational society. Both church and town remain, but the original scheme failed because of dissatisfaction, principally with a compulsory tax placed upon the holding of deeds, which was levied in support of the church.

A further example of the colonial influence on church building in Ohio is the Temple at Kirtland of the Reorganized Church of Latter-day Saints. The Temple, overlooking the village of Kirtland and the beautiful valley of the East Branch of the Chagrin River, was erected in 1834. It is described by Talbot Hamlin as being "unusual in its late use of extraordinarly rich Late-colonial type detail, especially in the interior." It was here that Joseph Smith, Jr., and his followers from Palmyra, New York, established themselves and drew many Mormon followers, extending the newly organized Church of Latter-day Saints.

The rectangular building is three stories high, surmounted by a colonial balustrade tower, lantern, and spire. Tradition has it that the women of the group broke up their glassware and china to mix with the stucco of the outside walls to give it a glistening effect. The most distinctive feature of the interior is a group of elevated pulpits, said to be unlike those of any other religious edifice in the world. Each group of pulpits consists of four tiers, for the grades of presiding officers, and each tier has three seats—making a twelvefold pulpit. There are two sets of these, on the east and west ends, set before the large central window of each wall. Before the front tier of pulpits is a leaf table that can be raised for the communion service.

The Temple was heralded at its dedication as a great

College First Church of God, Findlay, Ohio (B & J Photo Service)

achievement, in ceremonies lasting four days. Many marvelous signs were recounted as having been seen during the time. However, difficulties over land matters arose, and Smith and Rigdon, the leaders, were forced to leave the community in 1838. To satisfy a judgment the church was sold, and for a time served as a normal school. It was reopened as a place of worship in 1883 by the Reorganized Church of Latter-day Saints, which claimed to be the spiritual successor of Joseph Smith.

In Findlay, Ohio, The College First Church of God stands in imposing dignity. Although it was dedicated in 1950, this church marks a missionary effort which began a century earlier. It is the third church to take its impetus from the group founded in Harrisburg, Pennsylvania, by Elder John Winebrenner in 1830. This church, again, demonstrates religious development from a missionary effort to a modern church.

Grace Methodist Church in Dayton was originally a meeting house built in 1812 by one of the "circuit riders," the Reverend John Collins. This was later replaced by a brick structure, and the present church was erected in 1921. This is of Gothic design and at the time was named the "finest in all Methodism."

This church has served as a center of social organizations, and from it has spread the growth of Methodism in the territory. The building illustrates a transition from the meeting house to the more classic forms of architecture which characterize so many of the later churches erected in the Midwest. In this respect Grace Methodist Church took the first step forward from the pioneer to the more cultivated and elaborate style.

St. Joseph and The Child, St. Joseph's Church, Somerset, Ohio

In Cincinnati, an early center of religious activity originally called Losantiville, and a gateway to the West, there was an early Jewish congregation. Organized in 1824, this group was made up of English Jews who joined company with other immigrants from Holland and France. Later German Jews arrived, first swelling the group's number and eventually forming a separate congregation. This German congregation, under the rabbinate of Dr. Isaac M. Wise, built the famous Plum Street Temple in 1866, replacing an 1848 structure. This Temple was declared to be the "largest and most important structure of the kind in the United States."

The exterior walls are of gray brick, with extensive stone trim carved with floral designs in low relief. Two slender polygonal minarets rise above the roof in front; these are Moorish in design, a style which at the time had come into vogue in synagogue design. The interior is distinctly Byzantine, with brilliant gilding and arabesques, also in Moorish style. Today the building is chiefly a memorial, used for religious service only occasionally on special days.

The Catholic Church in Ohio has a long history. One of its earliest churches, called "the shrine of Catholicity in Ohio," is the Church of St. Joseph at Somerset.

Its presence in Ohio is the result of the entreaties of a layman, Jacob Dittoe, who in 1805, three years after Ohio was admitted into the Union, wrote to Bishop Carroll, the only bishop in the only diocese in the United States, asking that a priest be sent to minister to the settlers. He continued to write and implore until in 1808 a young Dominican priest, Father Edward Dominic Fenwick, visited the Dittoe family. He came yearly thereafter, and finally was authorized by the Bishop to settle there, which he did, until his consecration as bishop took him to Cincinnati in 1822.

St. Joseph (woodcarving), St. Joseph's Church, Somerset, Ohio

The original church of St. Joseph was built in 1818. A small log affair of no pretense, it was the first Catholic church opened and blessed in Ohio. It was also to become the Dominican foundation in the state, and a priory was established in conjunction with the church in 1836. The third, and present, structure was erected in 1866. The priory became a House of Studies in 1929.

It was from this church that much of the early Catholic missionary work proceeded, with the Dominican Fathers devoting themselves, as well, to the dissemination of education and culture. St. Joseph's, with its choir of Dominicans and its notable art pieces, remains an attractive, vital church even today, when the state may well boast of more elaborate church structures.

At the time of the Mississippi explorations, the territory which is now the State of Iowa was a rolling, green land, accessible and attractive to missionaries and new religious groups, many of whom traveled up-river from St. Louis. Lutheran, Amana, Catholic, and Congregational churches were among the many established by early Christian settlers in Iowa's villages and towns.

One quaint church in a small community has won renown far beyond its own rural boundaries. This is the First Congregational Church of Bradford, two miles northwest of Nashua, Iowa. Its claim to prominence is perhaps slight, but its appeal has been broad, for a song has been written about it—a song which invites all to "come to the church in the wildwood." It is a wooden church, built of local red oak timber; it has a bell cast "in Troy, N.Y.," which was rung almost continuously as it was transported to the church from Dubuque. The building was dedicated in 1864.

The story of the song is a simple one. The composer, William S. Pitts, had traveled to the prairie town of Brad-

"Little Brown Church in the Vale," Nashua, Iowa (Eris Studios)

ford by stagecoach on his way to visit his future wife at Fredericksburg. The year was 1857, and as the stagecoach was being readied to continue the journey, the young Mr. Pitts strolled out to the grove where the church now stands. The land had already been donated for the future church, but this was not generally known. Inspired by the scene, Mr. Pitts wrote the song after his return from his journey. Married to his lady the next year, it was six more years before he again traveled that way. It was then he discovered the church—the subject of his song, "The Church in the Wildwood." He sang the song in the church in 1864; it was published in 1865 and because of this the church has been called, and is most widely known as, "The Little Brown Church in the Vale."

Perhaps because of this nostalgic association, the church has been preserved though its survival seemed unlikely when the railroad by-passed Bradford in favor of another village. Today the church has thousands of visitors, and a thousand marriages, each year.

In another small town of Iowa stands a church designed by Martin Heer which is historic only because it has been given a unique title. This is the Catholic Church of St. Francis Xavier of Dyersville, which in 1956 was proclaimed a Basilica, a designation of honor and distinction, by Pope Pius XII.

In an Apostolic Brief, the Pontiff referred to the beauty of this Gothic building, the construction of which was begun in 1888: "The towering pinnacles of its twin spires reverently reach upward to heaven, while the interior of the church, strikingly spacious in its proportions, displays an elegance that befits its Gothic architecture; and its beauty is still further enhanced by paintings and statues of exquisite design and charm.

"Thus it is that those who are skilled in the arts do not

"Little Brown Church in the Vale," Nashua, Iowa (Eris Studios)

hesitate to include this church among the most distinguished of the country."

Beginning in the mid-seventeenth century, the land that is now the State of Wisconsin was a center of missionary activity by French Jesuits: René Menard, Marquette, and others. The French lost control of the territory in 1763, and British rule began. During the "missionary years" of the nineteenth century, churches were established in the state by Lutherans, Catholics, Episcopalians, Moravians, Congregationalists, and Methodists.

In considering missionary expansion in this state, one individual stands out as a "church builder" of excellence in these historic mission times. Father Samuel Charles Mazzuchelli, an Italian and a Dominican, was a missionary genius. A man of extraordinary vision and imagination, he alone designed and personally helped to build eighteen churches in the lead-mine district of northern Illinois and Wisconsin in the span of thirty-four years.

After the War of 1812, Wisconsin was freed of British influence, and actual occupation by the United States came in 1816 with the building of Fort Howard at Green Bay, and Fort Crawford at Prairie du Chien. It was not long afterward that the first permanent settlement in Wisconsin, originally named Natchez, but now the small town of New Diggings, was founded in 1824. The surrounding territory, because of the discovery of rich deposits of lead, became a mecca for miners. It was a new frontier, and immigrants came hurrying from East and South and abroad. Some, in their haste to obtain wealth, were too busy to build homes, and they burrowed into the hillsides.

Meanwhile Samuel Mazzuchelli, after completing his education in Europe, came to Cincinnati, Ohio, as a sub-deacon. There he was ordained a priest by Bishop Edward Fenwick,

St. Patrick's Church, Benton, Wisconsin

and was sent as a missionary into Michigan Territory, of
which Wisconsin was then a part. He worked first among the
Indians, then began his building work with the enlarging of
St. Anne's church in Green Bay. He built a first church in
that city, a frame building called St. John the Evangelist, and
opened the first Catholic school for white and Indian children in 1831, formulating a course of study which was ap-
proved by the National Indian Bureau.

Three years later Father Mazzuchelli, with the help of a
half-breed, Pierre Pacquette, built a chapel at Fort Winnebago, now Portage, the first chapel to be built in interior
Wisconsin since the Jesuits had departed one hundred and
fifty years earlier. He continued his work, building churches
in Dubuque, Iowa, and Galena, Illinois. At the opening
session of the first Wisconsin Territorial Legislative Assembly
at Belmont, Wisconsin, in 1836, he served as the first chaplain.
And the churches continued to rise.

One of the most notable of these churches still in use is
St. Patrick's Church at Benton, Wisconsin, built in 1845. It
is a stone structure of random ashlar, with Gothic touches
added to the distinctive marks of the designer and builder.
This church is perhaps the best extant example of Father
Mazzuchelli's architectural genius. It was here that he died
in 1864; his last words were, "How lovely are Thy taber-
nacles, O Lord of Hosts!"

A man of many abilities, Father Mazzuchelli was also a
practical, versatile man, and a faithful servant of his adopted
country. Besides his prodigious missionary efforts and his
genius for architecture, he taught, compiled a catechism for
the Winnebago Indians, published an almanac, and founded
a school for boys and a girls' academy.

Christ Episcopal Church, Boonville, Missouri (Toennes Studio)

THE WEST

The trek to the West is variously attributed to the prairie schooner, the stagecoach, homesteading, mining, and the laying of the iron rails. It is said to have reached its culmination in the driving of the "golden spike," which linked the rails of East and West to form the transcontinental railroad. But it was the "silver spikes"—the rising spires of churches—which symbolized the pioneers' achievement of permanence in the new land which had been opened to them.

The building of churches in the West was a gradual process, beginning in the late years of the missionary movement and reaching into the last years of the nineteenth century. No longer could the cowboy lament, "O Lord, I've never lived where churches grow . . ."

Settlers came from the East into the lands opened by the Louisiana Purchase in 1803. The churches, pioneering in the face of the lawless to claim "small plots for God" out of the vast acreages that were being quartered and sectioned to man's plow, followed the men who needed them. Here, removed from the refinements of the rapidly developing East, churchmen built with the means at hand—even building one church of baled hay which proved remarkably durable.

In the town of Altenburg, Missouri, a small Lutheran church was founded in 1839. The landowners round about decided in 1866 to build a more substantial church of stone. By then the Civil War was over, and a new wave of missions began, directed to the souls which now began rapidly to increase in number. Trinity Lutheran Church was modeled after the Roman style, built of umber-colored clay stone quarried locally. This is a soft stone which hardens when exposed to the weather. Oak timbers were hewn, and shingles cut from pine trees. The baptismal font was carved out of a single oak log. Most of the work was donated, and where

Christ Episcopal Church, Boonville, Missouri (Toennes Studio)

labor was the means of life itself, this offering was more precious than money.

In Boonville, Missouri stands Christ Church, an Episcopal church which had its beginning in the missionary years. The year 1835 marked a decided step forward in the organization of the Episcopal Church in the West. It was then that the Reverend Jackson Kemper of Connecticut was selected as the first missionary bishop of the church. In 1836 he selected Boonville as the center of his activity.

Organized as a church four years later, Christ Church was built in 1846, after having used a frame building for services. It was described at the time as presenting "one of the most beautiful specimens of church architecture to be found in the West—being sufficiently commodious for the largest congregation in this section of the country. It is constructed of brick . . . It is situated in a handsome and pleasant part of town." Christ Church is still hailed as the mother-church of the diocese.

Westward the trend continued, and at Lindsborg, Kansas, a group of pioneers met and founded Bethany Evangelical Lutheran Church, a crudely constructed church even for its time; but more pressing problems than esthetics confronted the pioneers of 1869. The first church building was of stone, with a grass roof and a bare earthen floor. It survived only five years; then a more substantial structure was put up. This remains, having been twice remodeled and enlarged.

Unique among its neighbors, this church is one of distinctive beauty. The chancel contains three large paintings. Two are by Birger Sandzen, one of which depicts Lazarus being raised from the dead, and the other Christ's Ascension. The third, by A. N. Malm, depicts Mary at the feet of Jesus. The church also has a beautifully carved altar and

Bethany Evangelical Lutheran Church, Lindsborg, Kansas

altar ring. The carpenter tools (precious among the pioneers) which were used to do this fine carving on the altar
had been brought from Sweden in a blue velvet box.

In Victoria, Kansas, one can see on the horizon a twin-
spired contrast to the level lands. This is the Catholic
Church of St. Fidelis, familiarly known as the "Cathedral
of the Plains." The territory was originally settled by Ger-
man-Russians who considered their church as necessary as
their homes. Their first church was a crude lean-to, built
against the side of one of the homes. This makeshift affair
was followed by a second building; a third was built on
acres of land donated by the Kansas Pacific Railroad. Later
settlers from Germany and from Ohio and Kentucky made
necessary the building of a fourth church, the present
"cathedral," begun in 1907.

St. Fidelis is a huge church, one of the largest between the
Mississippi and the Rockies. It is 220 feet in length, 73 feet
wide, and 107 feet wide at the transept. Its twin towers are
141 feet high, and its massive architecture is enhanced by
the level plains stretching out on all sides. It was, again, not
money alone which made this church possible—it was the
assessed and donated six loads of quarried limestone from
every parish member.

To the layman the amount of stone may mean nothing,
but any engineer can appreciate the fact that 125,000 cubic
feet of stone went into the building. Without power tools,
the stone, found in layers four feet below ground, were
hauled to the site in slabs eight feet long, there to be split
and dressed by hand. Each rock, weighing between 30 and
100 pounds, had to be handled individually and lifted into
place without automatic jacks or lifts. This "Cathedral of
the Plains," so splendid and built at such labor, is a "pyra-
mid to God," a testament of faith.

Cathedral of the Plains, Victoria, Kansas

The saga of the overland journey of the Church of Jesus Christ of Latter-day Saints is probably familiar to all. The unique aptness of its buildings, competing with the grandeur of mountains and valleys, is historic in itself. The "home" Temple at Salt Lake City, Utah, and its nearby Tabernacle are a culmination of the larger effort (see chapter on Cathedrals and Temples), but the churches in the smaller western towns are no lesser records of spiritual dedication. These churches span decades of building; and the program is not diminishing in force of execution. The whole concept is peculiarly western, for these churches (all called Temples) are spired records of energetic missionary enterprise.

We will list some of them briefly, giving but a few details of their design and structure:

St. George Temple, in the southwestern tip of Utah, was built in the years 1871 to 1877. More than a million feet of lumber was used, much of it being hauled by ox team a formidable distance of eighty miles; 17,000 tons of black volcanic rock and red sandstone were also used. In the course of excavation, springs were uncovered. Consequently, tons of rock fill were pounded into the foundation, the pounding being done by a hammer improvised from a lead-filled cannon used in the Mexican War.

Manti Temple, in Sanpete Valley, Utah, is built on a mountain of solid rock. Constructed in 1879 at a cost of a million dollars, it is a massive structure with walls three-and-a-half feet thick, buttresses four feet.

Logan Temple, in the northern part of Utah, took seven years to build—from 1877 to 1884. This Temple stands seven stories high, on an eight-acre plot, and is constructed of dark siliceous limestone.

Box Elder Stake Tabernacle, Brigham City, Utah, stands

Manti Temple, Sanpete Valley, Utah (*Deseret News Photo*)

against a background of high mountains that are capped with snow most of the year. In design this is an adaptation of the New England Puritan meeting house which incorporated Gothic details, as in windows and towers. The Tabernacle was constructed in 1876 of native lumber and stone, red sandstone and white wood, and labor was donated. The Temple has served as a missionary center.

The Cedar City First-Fifth Ward Chapel is a Mormon church made entirely of native materials. The colorful rocks and minerals are typical of the geological strata which, majestically exposed, are a part of southern Utah's scenic wonder. The builders created a colorful mosaic from approximately thirty kinds of stone which show different periods in the earth's history, particularly the Triassic and Jurassic periods of the Mesozoic era. Built in the years 1931 to 1934 by the cooperative effort of five hundred church members, it is a memorial of their enterprise during years of economic difficulty. Since its completion the church has been praised by geologists, artists, architects, and tourists.

More modern is the Temple of Idaho Falls, Idaho, completed in 1945. Its architecture is modern; the structural frame is heavy reinforced concrete, as are its walls. Its builders utilized the metals made plentiful by an industrial nation— copper, stainless steel, aluminum. But its foundation rests on volcanic lava bedrock.

The rugged land of Montana saw little church building until after the close of the "missionary period." In the state capital the Catholic Cathedral of St. Helena is a classically beautiful Gothic structure, its marble and stained glass serving to enhance the edifice which rises majestically among the surrounding mountains.

The Episcopal Church built its procathedral of St. Peter's

*Box Elder Stake Tabernacle, Brigham City, Utah
(courtesy D. W. Evans and Associates)*

in Helena in 1931 and while built in comparatively modern times, this procathedral has missionary interest. In the design of this Gothic building, the architects Whitehouse and Price of Spokane have shown a particular regard for the interior furnishings, achieving in their detail a combination of religious motifs and the history of the State of Montana. The stained glass windows contain allusions to both the Bible and Montana's past; the end panels of the altar of richly carved oak depict the evergreen, symbolizing immortality, and the bitter root, the state flower.

In simple, modernized Gothic style, the church is built of red porphyry stone taken from a nearby mountain, and the trimmings are of Indiana limestone. With its appropriately designed interior, this small classic church is a storehouse of symbols used both to instruct and to preserve the tradition of missionary work in the West.

Coming full sweep across the country, we again approach the Pacific coast, where the Spaniards spread their nets of missions. In San Francisco there is a much-loved church, Old St. Mary's—California's first cathedral. No longer the diocesan cathedral, this church, now served by the Catholic Order of Paulist Fathers, was built halfway up Nob Hill in the lusty, brawling, gay days when San Francisco was an infant. Built in 1854, St. Mary's has survived an exhausting past—the days of the Bonanza kings and the Railroad Four, and the Champagne Days, as San Franciscans called them (also known as the Gay Nineties). St. Mary's has stood through the Barbary Coast days and the rides of the Vigilantes, the encroachment of the red-light district, the tenements of Chinatown that crowded in. The building was shaken in the earthquake and damaged in the ensuing fire of 1906. It has known violence and witnessed the city's agony and shame—"its pews are dark with tears."

Cedar City First–Fifth Ward Chapel, Cedar City, Utah
(Church of Jesus Christ of Latter-day Saints)

Facing on St. Mary's Square, this old cathedral of California is a link between California's Catholic missions of the past and the church of today. Beautiful in its valiant service, in the objects of art that grace its interior, this church stands for the past and the future at the western portal of the United States.

*Idaho Falls Temple, Idaho Falls, Idaho
(courtesy D. W. Evans and Associates)*

V

SOME CATHEDRALS AND TEMPLES

Cathedrals and temples are, in two senses, the ultimate achievement in church building. First, every such edifice almost surely was preceded by one or more small churches of a territory or diocese which, through missionary activity and natural expansion, outgrew their modest bounds. The cathedral, in this sense, stands for spiritual achievement in the winning of a following large enough to warrant the erection of a capacious house of worship. Second, the planning and building of each cathedral and temple that stands was a labor of love. Into it went the determination that it be a thing of beauty. Whatever opinion the casual visitor may hold as to its style or esthetics, he must know that to those who built it, it represented the most splendid religious expression of which they were capable.

A criticism sometimes leveled at the architectural standards of democracies is that they are dictated by mass sentiment—

a taste for the "pretty" and "elegant" and a lack of appreciation for the truly beautiful. If we compare our creations with such rare wonders of the past as Solomon's Temple, the Parthenon, or the medieval cathedrals, we may feel that the charge is true. But if we limit our comparisons to our own era, we see that, while utility gets first consideration in our civic and industrial building, the striving toward expression of our own concept of beauty is evident in our great religious temples. The extravagant ruler who commissioned the greatest artists and architects of his day to produce the wonders of the past has never existed in this New World. Our religious monuments are the voluntary works of free men.

With all due respect to the glorious architectural forms of earlier days, from which we have borrowed freely, we have instilled our own concepts into each adopted style. (This subject will be considered further in the next chapter.)

We have built great churches in the United States. They are still being built, keeping pace with our country's material and spiritual growth.

The Cathedral of St. John the Divine in New York City will, when completed, be the largest Gothic cathedral in the world. It is now more than two-thirds finished. Work was begun with the laying of the cornerstone in 1892. The overall length of the Cathedral includes the majestic West Front with its Five Portals; the spacious narthex; the superb and perhaps unequaled nave; the Crossing in its still unfinished state. All lead up to the Great Choir, the Sanctuary, and the High Altar, around which are the towering columns and the Seven Ambulatory Chapels and the Baptistry.

The design of St. John the Divine is French Gothic. The architects have been: George L. Heins and C. Grant La Farge from July, 1891, until Mr. Heins' death in September, 1907;

Mr. La Farge from then until April, 1911; and Cram and Ferguson from April, 1911, to the present time.

The plan of the Cathedral is cruciform, with the head of the cross facing East. Seven chapels radiate from the apse, or semi-circular eastern end of the choir. The loftiest features of the elevation are the two towers of the West Front, 266.5 feet high, and the Flèche, or central spire, which will rise to an overall height of 452 feet.

The Cathedral extends from Amsterdam Avenue to Morningside Drive, more than a tenth of a mile. It is 601 feet long and will be 330 feet wide across the transepts, covering an area of 121,000 square feet. Its seating capacity will be about ten thousand, with standing room for many thousands more. It is being built entirely of stone; its core is Maine granite, its outer walls Mohegan granite from Peekskill, New York, and its inner surfaces are of Indiana limestone and Wisconsin dolomite. The only steel in its mighty frame is in the ridge of the nave roof, where in the old cathedrals wooden beams were used. Its foundations are in living rock, in some places 72 feet below the surface. St. John the Divine is built, like the pyramids, to stand for thousands of years.

To catalog the many details of superb art that, like facets of a gem, are gathered in this Cathedral, would be beyond the purpose or space of this book. One feature does, however, invite special attention. This is the Central Portal of the West Front, where the great bronze doors are to be seen. The principal detail of these doors is the sculpture of the panels, each of which contains a scene from the Old or New Testament. These doors weigh about twelve tons, and are eighteen-and-a-half feet high.

The great bronze doors occupy a distinguished, if not a singular, place in the annals of modern sculpture in America. In size, elaboration, and originality of design and cast, they stand as an extraordinary achievement. Henry Wilson was the

opposite: *Cathedral Church of St. John the Divine, New York City* (photo by A. Leonard Gustafson)

sculptor. For nearly three years he devoted himself to designing this memorial; they were his last work. Shortly after the
completion of the final models, he died. These doors represent one of the finest examples of this form of art in the
United States.

The Cathedral of St. John the Divine is hailed as "The
Word in Stone." Its stone carvings are like frozen music, its
every detail carefully planned and executed. It is a building
to be studied at length, for the carvings, tapestries, marble
sculptures, stained glass, and mosaics evoke in the observer
a sense of the juxtaposition of art, labor, and spirituality.

A well known and well loved landmark of New York City
is the famous St. Patrick's Cathedral , probably the most
famous Catholic church in the United States. It occupies a
city block bounded by Fifth and Madison Avenues and Fiftieth and Fifty-first Streets. It is the seat of the Roman Catholic
Archbishopric of New York.

The history of the Cathedral is an interesting one. In 1643
the first Catholic priest, the Jesuit martyr St. Isaac Jogues,
entered Manhattan seeking to convert the Mohawk Indians.
He was welcomed by the Dutch Governor, William Kieft,
and by the Dutch settlers of Nieuw Amsterdam. His mission
work flourished, but the first Catholic Church of the city,
St. Peter's, was not erected until 1785.

The site of the present St. Patrick's Cathedral was purchased in 1810, with the intention of building a college. In
1850 it was proposed that a cathedral be built, and in 1853
Archbishop John Hughes instructed the architect James
Renwick to prepare the studies and designs. The cornerstone
was laid in 1858. During the Civil War years construction
was suspended, but finally the work was completed, except
for the spires, in 1879. The spires were finished in 1888, the
Lady Chapel in 1906.

Bronze doors, St. John the Divine, New York City

Architecturally, the Cathedral is patterned after the Gothic style common in Europe from the thirteenth to the fifteenth centuries. Cologne and Rheims and some English cathedrals may be said to have furnished a prototype from which Mr. Renwick, an associate of Ralph Adams Cram, drew his inspiration for the distinctive design of St. Patrick's.

The foundation stones of the building are huge blocks of blue gneiss granite laid to ground level in cement mortar. A natural rock ledge rises nearly to the surface of Fifth Avenue, where the Cathedral's front entrance is situated; this ledge slopes east to a point some twenty feet below the surface of the south transept. Above the ground line, the first exterior base course of masonry is of Dix Island granite obtained from quarries in Maine. This granite also constitutes the first stone course under the columns and marble wall-surfaces of the interior of the Cathedral.

The whole exterior wall fabric is white marble, most of which was quarried at Pleasantville, New York. These walls are backed with brick and stone, rough masonry with hollow spaces to prevent dampness and aid ventilation. They are so well constructed that to this day no cracks have appeared in them.

The Cathedrals of St. Patrick and St. John the Divine are in the Gothic tradition. It may seem odd that the style and art of the Middle Ages have been widely revived in this young country, but it is certainly not regrettable. We see evolving an art all our own, but we can best develop a new tradition after we have studied, and practiced, the old ones.

We look now to another Gothic church which is not called a cathedral, but which, because of its majesty and size, might well be. This is the East Liberty Presbyterian Church of Pittsburgh, Pennsylvania. In 1819 an acre and a half of land was donated for the construction of a church. A brick church

St. Patrick's Cathedral, New York City
(Copyright 1942 by Archbishopric of New York)

and school were then built by the congregation. In 1930 Richard Beatty Mellon and Jennie King Mellon, his wife, proposed, in memory of their mothers, to erect and furnish a church building of monumental character. As a result, ground was broken for the new edifice in August, 1931, and the work was completed five years later.

Writing of this church of Gothic design, Ralph Adams Cram spoke for its architects: "Here the donors had a vision of adequacy and completeness; the architects that ideal which is so seldom to be realized; and the coalition of those two factors has resulted in a monument that reveals the working out of this complete community of desires and ideals. It is doubtful if there is anywhere in this country a church of similar magnitude where every detail of utility and artistic quality has been achieved in so full a degree. In saying this, the architects make no estimate of the aesthetic quality of the work, only of the completeness which has been achieved.

"In this they have had the cordial cooperation of those allied artists without whom mere architecture would fail of its effect. Sculptors, craftsmen in stained glass, metal workers of every sort, cabinet makers, wood carvers, all have been of the highest standard of capacity the time affords. Their work speaks for itself. So the East Liberty Church stands as a complete epitome of all the ecclesiastical arts, recovered out of the great centuries of vital religious art, and made operative again in a new day and generation.

"Architecturally, a sincere effort has been made to achieve something of this same unity, consistency and significance. The general style is Gothic, of course, for this was the supreme expression of Christian civilization brought into being to express in the fullest degree the ethos and the operation of the Christian religion. On the other hand, no effort has been made to obtain archeological exactitude. The design follows no definite precedent nor is it based on any ancient church

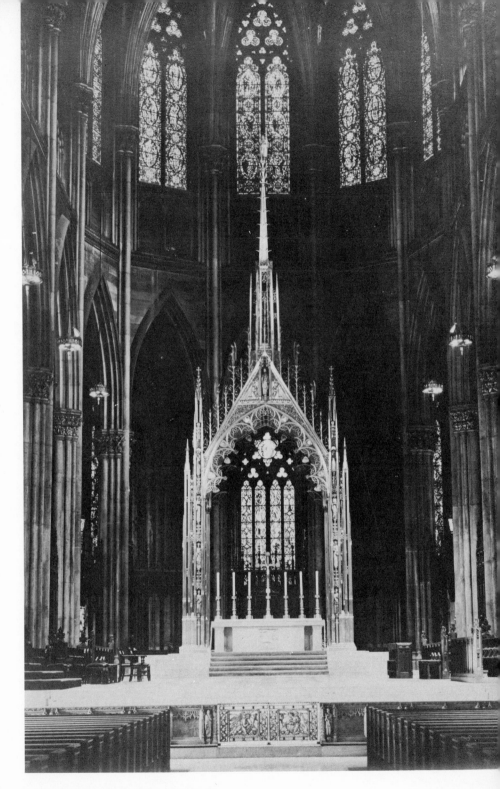

St. Patrick's Cathedral, New York City
(Copyright 1942 by Archbishopric of New York)

already existing. You may find in it, if you like, suggestions from France, England, Spain, indeed from any place where Gothic was a living force—but suggestions only. These qualities have been used only as, so to speak, building material out of which something new, the architects believe, has been developed; something new that is also, in its essential quality, the old. This is a statement of intent and aspiration, not necessarily of accomplishment."

East Liberty Church did not establish a trend—but it has added to our rich store of one of the world's most splendid genres.

Another cathedral-like church, though not so designated, is the Riverside Church in New York City, which can trace its history to the First Baptist Church, founded in New York in 1762. Its direct lineage goes back to February 13, 1841, when a small congregation built the Norfolk Street Baptist Church.

While the present church is an extremely impressive one, its history is filled with difficulties and disappointments. The economics of building and running the early Baptist churches were very nearly beyond the capacities of their congregations. When the Norfolk Street church burned to the ground seven years after it was built, its young preacher, Thomas Armitage, conducted services in the Rutgers Female Institute for two years. The new church, built in 1850, had a debt of thirty thousand dollars; but it also had a gifted preacher, probably the more inspired when he realized the importance of drawing great crowds each Sunday. By 1859 this enterprising pastor determined that a larger church was necessary and bought five lots on Fifth Avenue. The Fifth Avenue Church was built in 1860. During the Civil War the church suffered severely. Dr. Armitage was nearly killed in the draft riots of 1863, and financial trouble forced the congregation to sell the church lots the same year.

When Dr. Armitage suggested building a "meetinghouse" in 1864 he was thought quite unrealistic, but his courage rallied the group; within a year a new Fifth Avenue Baptist Church was built. A debt of fifty thousand dollars now faced the church. The young William Rockefeller then suggested the organization of a sinking fund. Between Rockefeller and J. A. Bostwick, the debt was paid by 1878.

The next church to be built in this progression was the Park Avenue Baptist Church, completed in the spring of 1922. Its pastor, Dr. Cornelius Woelfkin, had begun his ministry in 1912 at the Fifth Avenue Church, and had to wait until after the World War to see the new building completed.

It is here that the story of The Riverside Church itself begins. Dr. Woelfkin became ill shortly after the Park Avenue Church was completed, and the officers of the church followed the pastor's advice to find a replacement for him. They chose to invite the controversial Dr. Harry Emerson Fosdick, then at the First Presbyterian Church in New York, to take over their congregation. Dr. Woelfkin, like some of his predecessors, was a man of liberal mind; so was Dr. Fosdick.

Harry Emerson Fosdick agreed to take the pastorate on condition that the church admit to membership Christians of all denominational backgrounds—requiring only their affirmation of faith in Christ—while retaining its own historic denominational affiliation. He further required that a new and larger building be erected. The conditions were agreed to, and Dr. Fosdick's ministry began in 1925.

The building committee worked with the architects Charles Collens and Henry C. Pelton, who selected as their model the Gothic-style Chartres Cathedral. The cornerstone of The Riverside Church was laid on November 27, 1927, and, after considerable destruction by fire the following year, the building was at last opened for the first Sunday service on October 5, 1930.

The opening was impressive indeed. More than six thousand people sought admission; Dr. Fosdick spoke of the sobering beauty of the church, whose interior was rich in stained glass, a white Caen stone chancel screen, a gilded cross and candle bearers on the altar. Liberalism was the keynote of its iconography, which was worked in stained glass and sculpture: in the chancel screen, St. Luke of the Physicians panel was flanked by Louis Pasteur, Sir Joseph Lister, and others; Christ as Teacher was depicted with Socrates, Erasmus, and Pestalozzi. The themes of the stained glass aisle windows were modern, dealing with agriculture, government, scholarship, and such. Most startling of all, carved into the arches of the West Portal were the great philosophers, religious leaders, and scientists—Descartes, Spinoza, Kant, Confucius, Buddha, Mohammed, Darwin, Pasteur, Einstein. John D. Rockefeller, Jr., provided the tower—twenty-two floors of office space and meeting rooms—at the pinnacle of which is the great belfry which houses the seventy-three-bell Laura Spelman Rockefeller Memorial Carillon. Two floors below street level were fitted with bowling alleys, a gymnasium, auditorium, stage, and kitchens.

Responsible persons deeply involved with this venture knew that the richness of the church would never compensate for lack of vitality, but they soon found that an active role was open to it. During the depression, a unique relief program assisted thousands to find employment through a special personnel service initiated by the church. The Social Service Department of the church was begun at this point, and continues today.

Today The Riverside Church is known as a vital, beautiful

Islamic Center, Washington, D. C.

landmark to everyone who knows, lives in, or visits New York City.

Our national capital has many buildings of great historic significance and magnificent proportions. And it has great churches, the greatest of which are now being completed or have recently been dedicated. The National Shrine of the Immaculate Conception, begun with the laying of the cornerstone in 1920, is at last nearly finished. This church is of Byzantine-Romanesque design, and while it is large and splendidly executed, its fittings, mosaics, and works of art are less impressive than the fact that this vast undertaking was underwritten by Catholic parishioners of churches across the country.

Washington, D. C., as the capital of a great nation, is a place of international importance. For many years Muslims· had felt a need for an Islamic cultural and religious center in the United States. Finally, in 1945, some of the prominent Muslim-Americans met with the ambassadors from Muslim countries and began practical work on the idea. Construction of the building did not begin until 1949. The Islamic Center was completed and dedicated in the summer of 1956. It stands at the corner of Massachusetts Avenue and Belmont Road in northwest Washington.

The design of the building was created by the Egyptian Ministry of Wakfs, executed by an American architect, Mr. Irvin S. Porter, and supervised by an American Muslim builder, Mr. A. J. Howar.

The Mosque, the Islamic church, is the most important part of the Center. It is situated at an angle facing in the direction of Mecca, Saudi Arabia. Inside the Mosque are beautiful materials gathered from many countries; among these are Turkish tiles, an Egyptian chandelier and an Egyp-

Washington Cathedral, Washington, D. C.
(from a water color by E. Donald Robb. Photo by Horydczak)

tian pulpit, Iranian carpets, and Vermont marble around the columns. All of these materials are gifts from their respective countries. Egypt also sent three highly skilled and specialized artists who painted the ceiling and the walls.

A small arched alcove is situated in the center of the interior front wall of the Mosque. This is called a "Mehrab," and indicates the direction in which lies the Holy Kaaba in the city of Mecca. It is interesting to note that there is absolutely no religious significance attached to any of the designs used to decorate the interior of the Mosque: columns, windows, walls, and so on. All of the designs are purely decorative for the beautification of the room. Of course, the Arabic words inscribed on the walls and ceiling have religious significance in that they are verses from the holy Koran, and the various Names and Titles of God.

A lecture hall with a capacity of three hundred is located in the basement of the Mosque. Here periodic lectures on Islamic culture, on religious subjects in general, and on Muslim literature, philosophy and art, are given by both Muslim and non-Muslim scholars.

The Mosque is flanked by two large wings, at the front of the courtyard, which house the Islamic Institute. The wing on the right contains the offices of the Director and his staff, and that on the left houses the library. The Center, built of Alabama limestone, occupies about thirty thousand square feet. Topped by a slender and beautiful minaret, the Islamic Center is intended to be a symbol of alliance between the Crescent and the Cross.

There is now being completed in our nation's capital what will probably be the most magnificent church structure and historic monument ever to be constructed in America. This is the Washington Cathedral (Cathedral of St. Peter and St. Paul). It stands on a fifty-seven acre stretch of land on the

opposite: Washington Cathedral, Washington, D. C.
(photo by Severance)

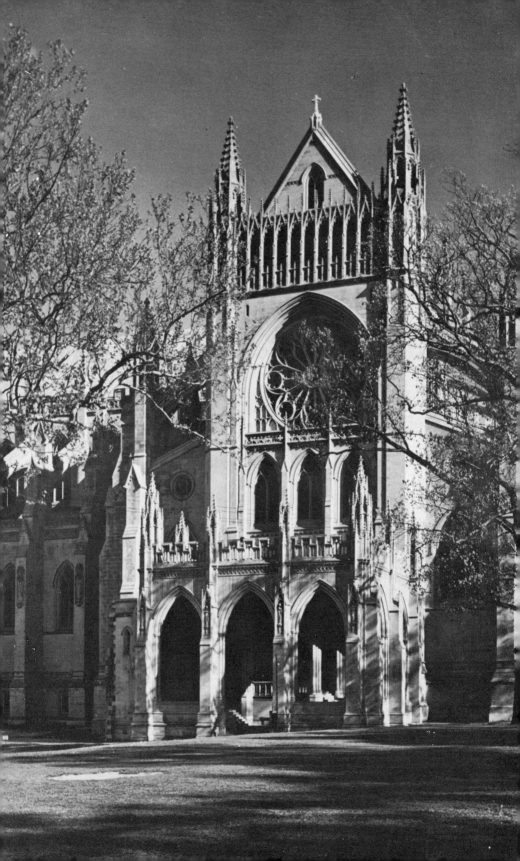

crest of Mount St. Alban's, where the Cathedral Close presents a landscape resplendent with flowers, trees, and lawn.

The Cathedral had a historic beginning. President George Washington had spoken hopefully of a great church for all the people of the nation. The idea remained only an idea until, in 1893, the charter of Washington Cathedral was granted to a group of laymen by the Congress of the United States. The Cathedral's constitution obligates it to serve as a "House of Prayer for all people, forever free and open, welcoming all who enter its doors . . ."

And in 1903 the Congress recognized the Protestant Episcopal Cathedral Foundation, empowering it to "establish and maintain within the District of Columbia a cathedral and institutions of learning for the promotion of religion and education and charity." In 1907 the cornerstone of the Cathedral was laid.

At the present time Washington Cathedral is more than sixty percent finished. The final estimated cost of construction is eighteen million dollars. No date can be set for its completion. It is being built and maintained, as a national shrine, entirely by the free will offerings and gifts of its friends of many denominations throughout the United States. When completed, it will be one tenth of a mile long and rank sixth in area (75,000 square feet) among the cathedrals of the world.

Although Washington Cathedral is chartered as a foundation of the Protestant Episcopal Church, five denominations now worship there regularly: Protestant Episcopal, Russian Orthodox, Temple Sinae Jewish Congregation, Polish National Catholic, and St. Andrew's Ukrainian Orthodox. Each Sunday, according to Cathedral tradition, one of the forty-eight states or territories is honored in Washington Cathedral, with special prayers offered for the life and work of the people of the state.

Washington Cathedral, Washington, D. C.   (photo by Horydczak)

The Cathedral is built in pure Gothic design; its architect is Philip Hubert Frohman. Constructed to outlast all other buildings in Washington, experts give it at least three thousand years. But its quality of permanence is not so immediately impressive as are the richness, the artistry, the quiet beauty of its interior. Its stained glass windows, presenting figures in our national history, Biblical scenes, and Christian heroes and saints, are enchantingly beautiful, as are the carvings, statues, and stonework which seem living representations of flora and fauna of the earth. Its towers will rise 107 feet above the tip of the Washington Monument.

Its memorials, like its dimensions, are grand in concept.

We single out two of the historic memorials which will give the Cathedral a place as a national shrine as well as a church. These are the statues of George Washington and Abraham Lincoln. The heroic sculpture of our first president stands, temporarily, in the west aisle of the transept. The figure is seven-and-a-half feet tall and was sculpted from white Vermont marble by Lee Lawrie.

Just inside the parclose arch is a kneeling figure of Abraham Lincoln. It is believed to be the only statue of the Great Emancipator in an attitude of prayer. It was executed by Herbert Honck of Harrisburg, Pennsylvania, whose grandfather, while walking through the fields near Gettysburg, once discovered Lincoln kneeling in the leaves. This recollection of his grandfather was the sculptor's inspiration for this reverent memorial.

The areas of ecclesiastical jurisdiction of the Catholic Church are dioceses, each of which has its see church, or cathedral. Many Catholic churches are distinguished with the title of "Cathedral," and among them are some of historic distinction. In this section we shall look at a few of these, located

Cathedral of St. Peter in Chains, Cincinnati, Ohio
(Telegraph-Register)

in the Midwest, because they have features of general interest.

While it is no longer the diocesan cathedral, nor the seat of the bishop, the procathedral of St. Joseph's of Bardstown, Kentucky has a memorable place in history. Three years after the Reverend Benedict Joseph Flaget was named bishop of the newly created diocese of Bardstown in 1816, the Cathedral of St. Joseph was dedicated. It was the third cathedral to be built in what is now the United States, the other two being in Baltimore and New Orleans.

The Cathedral is classical in design, a combination of Roman and Grecian influences with emphasis on the Romanesque. Its front portico is supported by six Doric columns, while its vaulted ceiling and interior columns are of the Tuscan order and thus Roman in style. The tower which surmounts the building is a separate structure of German derivation but also of the Romanesque period. It was built of materials of the vicinity, and is said to be structurally faultless. St. Joseph's Cathedral has been selected by the Advisory Committee of the Historic-American Building Survey of the Department of the Interior as a historical building. It was designed and built by the architect John Rodgers, who was also a wood-carver and musician.

Most notable among the memorials and possessions of St. Joseph's procathedral are nine paintings which were a gift to the church by King Louis Philippe of France. As the Duke of Orleans, before becoming King, Louis Philippe had visited Bardstown in 1797 on his travels to New Orleans with his two brothers. After some litigation over their import, duty-free, "being for the sole use of the church," the paintings arrived late in 1822. The art works are: Jan van Eyck's *Annunciation* and *Descent of the Holy Ghost;* Murillo's *Coronation of the Blessed Mother; St. Peter in Chains, St. John the Baptist,* and *The Winged St. Mark,* all by Van

Old Cathedral of St. Louis, St. Louis, Missouri

Dyck; *St. Aloysius Teaching,* by an unknown artist; Rubens'
Flaying of St. Bartholomew; and *The Crucifixion,* by van
Bree.

Another church which was originally the diocesan cathedral is St. Peter in Chains, in Cincinnati, Ohio. It is the most
impressive example of Greek Revival architecture in the city,
and is located at the corner of Eighth and Plum Streets. The
architect was Henry Walter, who is better known as the designer of the Ohio State Capitol in Columbus. The cornerstone of the old cathedral was laid in 1841, and the dedication
took place in 1845.

The building is a grand monument, measuring 200 feet by
80 feet with an interior height of 55 feet. Thus the ground
dimensions are only a little smaller than those of the Parthenon in Athens. The architect emphasized Greek simplicity in
the clean sweep of the outer walls. Though sturdily built,
and hailed at its completion as "the finest building in the
West," and "the most imposing in appearance," the cathedral
has been little appreciated. It was not maintained well, and
not until 1956 was a serious attempt made to renovate and
preserve this structure. It is now completely refurbished at
a cost of four million dollars (the original cost of the building was $120,000), and the new stained glass, the work of
Emil Stoettner, is among the finest in contemporary America.

St. Raphael Cathedral of Dubuque, Iowa, was completed
in 1861, replacing a previous cathedral built by the missionary "church builder," Father Samuel C. Mazzuchelli, O.P.
Tradition has it that he also drew the plans of the present
Cathedral, but, when he went elsewhere in his work, the final
construction was carried on by a man named Egan from
Chicago. Originally the interior was of Gothic design, a

New Cathedral of St. Louis, St. Louis, Missouri

miniature of Notre Dame in Paris. The Cathedral is built of brick, native stone, and metal.

St. Raphael's stained glass windows were cast in London in 1886, and are considered works of art. There are eight double windows on either side, each having life-size images of subjects from the Old Testament and the Christian era. Over the altar is a great fresco which represents the final establishment of the Christian Church on earth in the descent of the Holy Spirit upon the Apostles. Paintings by Gregori of Florence, Italy, are on the walls of the nave, and depict the great doctors and fathers of the church.

In the city of St. Louis, Missouri, are two outstanding cathedral buildings. The Old Cathedral, the third church to be built on the site, was dedicated in 1834. No longer the cathedral church of the Archdiocese, it is today the parish church of the parish of St. Louis IX, King of France, and is located at Second and Walnut Streets.

The city of St. Louis was visited as early as 1672 by the missionary priest, Father Marquette. Its first parish, that of Ste. Genevieve, was organized in 1749. But before that a French trading post had been set up there by Pierre Laclède Liguest and Auguste Chonteau. Later, Laclède declared the site to be one on which might well grow "one of the most beautiful cities in America." Drawing plans for the future town, Laclède dedicated a square on the river-front as the site of a future church.

The Old Cathedral is the oldest cathedral building west of the Mississippi River. It has had a history of great and minor events. In May, 1849, the steamboat *White Cloud* caught fire and set the city ablaze. A captain of volunteer firemen, Thomas B. Torgee, in a desperate but eventually successful attempt to save the Old Cathedral, lost his life when a discharge of gunpowder went off prematurely. However, it was

New Cathedral of St. Louis, St. Louis, Missouri

his heroic effort which saved the building that survives to the present day.

The Old Cathedral is the most highly indulgenced church in America. It was here in 1845 that the first Conference of the Society of St. Vincent de Paul in the United States was organized. While all the other buildings along the old riverfront area have been demolished, the Old Cathedral will remain as part of the Jefferson Memorial Park in St. Louis.

The Old Cathedral of St. Louis served until it was felt that the building was no longer adequate for the city's needs. Its successor was begun in 1903 with the purchase of land on the corner of Lindell Boulevard and Newstead Avenue in the western part of the city. The New Cathedral is Byzantine in design.

As it stands today the Cathedral is the result of a building process that has been carried on since May 1, 1907, when the first earth was turned by Archbishop John J. Glennon. The cornerstone was laid on October 18, 1908, and the work had progressed sufficiently for services to be held in the new building by October, 1914.

St. Louis Cathedral has a majestic exterior. It dominates the city's western horizon and challenges the passerby with its great mass and the harmonious proportions of its lines. Its most striking feature, in keeping with its Byzantine style, is its huge central dome, which towers, with its surmounting cross, 227 feet above street level.

The most remarkable of the Cathedral's luxuriant interior decorations are the mosaics. These mosaics are now reputed to be the most valuable collection in the world. Both stones and glass are used. A layer of pure gold leaf is placed on glass and covered with a very thin glass film. The pressed glass is then cut in very small cubes, or tesserae, about a half-inch square; these pieces are used in conjunction with colored tesserae and stones to produce a picture. The colorful stones

St. Paul Cathedral, St. Paul, Minnesota (photo by Riehle Studios)

that are used are cut in irregular shapes and placed at various angles, giving almost infinite variability to the effects achieved by different tones and angles of light. Some ten thousand different shades of color are found in the mosaics of this Cathedral, and it has been estimated that more than one hundred million pieces of stone and glass were used in the completion of these great expanses of art.

From the viewpoint of magnificence and richness of decoration, St. Louis Cathedral is recognized to be the foremost church of the Americas done in the Byzantine style.

In the Catholic archdiocese of St. Paul, Minnesota, near the headwaters of the Mississippi River, stands the magnificent Cathedral of St. Paul.

The story of the Cathedral began in 1841 when a little log chapel was erected on the banks of the Mississippi and dedicated to St. Paul, the Apostle. Minnesota became a state seventeen years later, and its capital city adopted the saint's name. The second Cathedral, a brick structure, was erected in 1851, and the third, of stone, was built in 1858. The project of building the present Cathedral was decided upon by Archbishop John Ireland in March, 1904. Construction began two years later on a site rising above the city, on Summit Avenue, and the church was opened for services in March, 1915. Interior decoration continues to the present day.

The architect of St. Paul Cathedral was Mr. E. L. Masqueray, who died in 1917. In style it is Classical Renaissance, its main feature being a majestic dome. The Cathedral is built of granite from the quarries of St. Cloud, Minnesota, and varieties of marble from many parts of the world. One of the largest church buildings of the North American continent, the Cathedral is 307½ feet high, 381 feet long and 216 feet wide. It has a seating capacity of four thousand.

The façade of St. Paul Cathedral has many sculptured

St. Paul Cathedral, St. Paul, Minnesota (photo by Riehle Studios)

forms; among others, above the main archway we see the figure of Christ, the Apostles grouped around Him. The text carved below these figures recalls the mission founding of the city: "Going therefore teach ye all nations."

The interior of the Cathedral imparts a sense of elevation of spirit. Here the objective of the architect was to "compose space harmoniously." Two features of the interior are worthy of special mention. The altar is monumental, surmounted by a canopy or baldachin supported on six huge columns of black and gold Portora marble. Each of these columns is a monolith, a single stone; they stand together like six "black-robes." The splendid baldachin of Verona marble and bronze was designed by Whitney Warren of New York.

The other notable feature is the series of seven bronze grilles set in a half-circle between the piers back of the altar. Extending along the top surface of the grilles is a frieze, also of bronze, of full-size figures presenting seven episodes in the life of St. Paul. The grilles are exactly the same on both sides, every ornament, face, and symbol appearing in reverse from the opposite side. Thus, while done in silhouette, all features and figures have a three-dimensional or fully rounded effect. Sculpted by E. H. Atkins of Boston and cast locally, this work is unique—nowhere else in the world is there a work in bronze of similar scale and spirit.

Like other great cathedrals, that of St. Paul has many memorial pieces and outstanding works of art. It is a truly great accomplishment, particularly when we consider that little more than a hundred years separate our missionary days from so laudable an achievement in church building.

It was just before the close of the nineteenth-century missionary period that the Mormons settled in the West, notably in Utah. Almost immediately they began work on two structures of cathedral-like proportions and splendor.

The Salt Lake City Temple is a monument as well as a temple. Four days after the arrival of the Mormon settlers at a barren site in the heart of what is now Salt Lake City, Brigham Young, the leader, was walking with his associates. Suddenly he stopped, and, striking the point of his cane in the ground, exclaimed, "Here we will build the Temple of our God." The spot was noted, and that evening a square of ten acres was marked out for the Temple Block. The city was planned around this square, rather in the pattern of a checkerboard, with ten-acre blocks laid out around the Temple area. Unusually wide streets, 120 to 132 feet across, separated the blocks.

Construction on the Temple began in 1853. Truman O. Angel was the original architect, but in 1883, with the structure half finished, another architect, Joseph Don Carlos Young, completed the work and designed the interior.

Building of this Temple took precedence over all other considerations, even though the people were nearly destitute and living in a strange arid land where even the probability of survival was sometimes doubtful. As Brigham Young counseled, "I want to see the Temple built in a manner that will endure through the Millennium. I want that Temple to stand as a proud monument of the faith, perseverance and industry of the Saints of God in the mountains, in the nineteenth century."

The Salt Lake City Temple is 186½ feet in length, 118½ feet wide, and 210 feet high at the central tower. The wall thicknesses are from six to nine feet. The total area is 4,850 feet. Atop the highest pinnacle stands the Angel Moroni, from the Book of Mormon, a statue of hammered copper covered with gold leaf sculptured by Cyrus E. Dallin.

The architecture of the building, while it may be said to have certain "contemporary" aspects from the principle of "form following function," is a composite of various derived architectural forms. It has been described as of Romanesque adaptation.

The Salt Lake City Temple was constructed in the same spirit as were the temples of antiquity. The costliest materials obtainable, precious stones, china, fine glass and metals were placed in the Temple. In the dedicatory prayer, President Wilford Woodruff referred to the "ornamentation . . . the painting and plastering, the gilding and bronzing, the fine work in wood and metal, of every kind, the embroidery and needlework, the pictures and statuary, the carved work and canopies . . ."

Dedicated on April 6, 1892, the Temple had been opened a day earlier to non-Mormon visitors. Since its dedication, however, only those of the faith who live up to the standard of moral and spiritual conduct required of its membership have been admitted to the building.

Another Mormon building stands near the Temple in Salt Lake City. This is the Tabernacle, a building with a great oval roof that has attracted world-wide interest since its completion. The Tabernacle accommodates most of the General Conferences of the Church of Jesus Christ of Latter-day Saints, as well as a number of other religious gatherings. It has a seating capacity of eight thousand. It is more than a religious center, however, serving also as a cultural center. The great artists of the world have sung and played there, and leading figures, including Presidents of the United States and leading clergymen of various faiths, have spoken there.

As a religious structure, the Tabernacle has no architectural antecedents. It is 250 feet long, 150 feet wide, and 80 feet high. The massive roof is supported only by great wooden arches which span the width of the building. The Tabernacle was constructed at a time and under conditions that precluded the use of steel girders and tie-rods. It is really a great

Salt Lake City Temple, Salt Lake City, Utah
(Church of Jesus Christ of Latter-day Saints)

bridgework of latticed timbers fastened together with large wooden pins. This truss-work occupies a space of ten feet from the inside plastered ceiling to the outside roofing.

The roof rests like a great inverted bowl on forty-four pillars or buttresses of cut sandstone masonry, each measuring nine feet from the outside to the inside of the building. Each of these pillars is three feet thick, and they range from 14 to 20 feet high. The spaces between the buttresses are occupied for the most part by large doors, permitting rapid egress from the building.

Construction work on the Tabernacle was begun on September 1, 1865, and religious services were held there in 1867. No plans for the structure exist, the architects having directed the work in the time-honored tradition of the master builder. According to Levi Edgar Young, Brigham Young and his counselors had given careful consideration to the subject of building a larger "meetinghouse."

The plan for the Tabernacle was suggested by Brigham Young, and William H. Folsom and Henry Grow were chosen to direct its construction. Brigham Young wanted a building without interior columns, and of the schemes proposed to achieve this, the one by Henry Grow was accepted.

Henry Grow had been a bridge builder in Pennsylvania, and had used lattice trusses in these bridges. He had recently spanned, with a lattice truss, a river west of Salt Lake City, and proposed an adaptation of this truss to span the meetinghouse. Brigham Young thought this the most logical possibility, and Grow and Folsom were given the responsibility of erecting the Tabernacle.

The roof was originally covered by wooden shingles; in about 1900 a metal covering was superimposed, and recently the roof was replaced by aluminum. The accuracy of workmanship which had gone into the building was made evident during the application of this aluminum roof. The contrac-

Salt Lake Tabernacle, Salt Lake City, Utah
(photo by Hal W. Rumel)

tor reported to the church architect, Edward O. Anderson, that his instrument check showed less than a quarter-inch tolerance in alignment. The new roof, therefore, was applied with considerable ease.

The gallery inside the building was added in 1870. Measuring 30 by 390 feet and resting upon 72 columns, it afforded additional seating for two thousand. It is reported that the acoustics of the building were actually aided by this addition, though the columns did not improve vision from the sides.

In Wilmette, Illinois, just north of Chicago, is an unusual and beautiful temple, the first of its kind in the United States. It is known as the Bahai House of Worship. Following the constructive, humane teachings of the Founder of the Bahai World Faith, which originated in Persia in the mid-nineteenth century, a small group of his followers determined to build a temple. They had no funds, owned no property, had no architectural plan in mind—but they made a beginning. From that beginning evolved what has been called Chicago's Taj Mahal.

The first step was a competition held for the purpose of securing a design, and in 1920 a meeting at the national Bahai convention in New York was called to give consideration to the submitted plans. Three designs were offered in the usual form of drawings and renderings. One other, however, was presented in a plaster model on which the French-Canadian architect, Louis J. Bourgeois, had worked for three years. The delegates were pleased with this work, for it represented their dreams of form, symbol, and ornamentation. Before reaching a decision, however, they consulted H. Van Buren Magonigle, later president of the New York Chapter of the American Institute of Architects, who gave this opinion: "The architect has conceived a Temple of Light in which structure, as usually understood, is to be concealed, visible

Bahai House of Worship, Wilmette, Illinois

support eliminated as far as possible, and the whole building to take on the airy fabric of a dream. . . . It is the first new idea in architecture since the thirteenth century."

In 1921 the caissons for the building were sunk down to bedrock, and the foundation basement for the future temple was completed. For about ten years no further progress was made. This enabled the Bahais to gather the funds necessary for the next stage of construction. And it gave the engineers time to solve some unprecedented construction problems.

The major difficulty lay in translating Bourgeois' magnificent design into structural form. This was finally solved by John J. Earley, an architectural sculptor of Washington, D.C., shortly before the death of the architect. Earley developed a method of using cement as a plastic material and casting it in forms; the pattern for each form was first cut in plaster by sculptors. Earley also worked out a formula for casting a mixture of white cement and ground crystalline quartz in the sculptured molds. The resulting sections of cast stone were hung piece by piece as the permanent ornamentation for the Temple.

Work on the superstructure began in 1930. In structure the Temple is actually a great concrete, steel, and glass building, to which, both inside and out, has been applied the plastic-type, pre-cast stone. In June, 1932, the task of applying the ornamentation to the superstructure was started. One section at a time was finished, as funds became available. In January, 1943, all of the exterior, including the steps, was finished.

During World War II no further work was undertaken. Then in January, 1947, work was begun on the interior. The same kind of material used for the exterior of the Temple was chosen. Landscaping of the grounds was started in April, 1952. On May 2, 1953, the dedication ceremony was held.

Bahai House of Worship, Wilmette, Illinois

The Temple, which stands on a plot of land of nearly seven acres, seats twelve hundred. Its total cost, including landscaping, is approximately three million dollars.

Because the design is unusual, attempts have been made to find a single descriptive term for the Temple's architectural style. Some observers point out traces of different styles: Egyptian, Romanesque, Arabic, Renaissance, Byzantine. By suggestions of these various styles, Bourgeois indicated the repeated efforts of men to glorify God. Although individuals may see various meanings in the architecture and design, the essential thing is that the Temple stands for unity. Each Bahai Temple has nine sides; this is the only architectural requirement in the Bahai teachings.

The auditorium of the Temple is open to all people for prayer and meditation. No race or religion is barred. The seats in the central part of the auditorium face the Holy Land. Above the heads of the worshipers, in the apex of the dome, is the symbol of the Greatest Name. This is an invocation to God in Arabic script which may be translated as "O Glory of the All Glorious."

While the Bahai religion came to the United States rather recently, in 1893, it has progressed to the building of its Temple at Wilmette in a comparatively short time. The exterior, interior, grounds, and unique fittings of this Temple form an unusual, and historic, attainment in church structure.

Cathedrals and temples, as accomplishments which reflect a concerted will toward an ideal, are extensions of the age-old realization that the spirit of the people is awakened and uplifted by a work of beauty. In the magnificence of every American cathedral we should see the beauty of the many churches which inspired its growth.

Bahai House of Worship, Wilmette, Illinois

VI

MODERN CHURCHES

Church membership in the United States is steadily increasing. Obviously, this growth must be accommodated, and the only means of achieving this end is to build more churches. And here we recognize the existence of an opportunity to develop an indigenous architecture in a field in which, more than in any other, the traditional has persistently been held to, or, at least, imitated.

There are those who demand a new expression in church architecture; by some, its coming is regretted. But there is evidence even now, in the best of the modern church designs, that the United States will produce in the future a distinctive architectonic form. While the new style will not be a severance from the traditional and classic forms, it will utilize the new materials and techniques we have developed. The result will be an evolvement of structural adaptation into which is blended the intrinsic beauties of new materials.

Surely, the development of any new form requires a period of preparation and experimentation. But, although we may consider that we are now progressing through such a period, we have faltered in two ways: First, we have tried to make haste too quickly, applying "novel" devices of structural art and thinking ourselves progressive. True, there must be some testing ground. In the chapel and the petite church we can try the wings of new expression. The danger lies, however, in that a curiosity may become a fad which tomorrow's historians will deplore in evaluating the esthetics of our time.

Second, it is known from abundant example that the insight of the artist is essential to a harmonious church structure and its appointments. Here again, haste to produce something "new" has usurped the place of careful preparation. Because of the use of imitation art in churches, mass-produced to satisfy the growing demand, artists have been eager to give expression to their own concepts of what "modernity" should be—many of them without training either in the fundamentals of visual art or in religious concepts. The result is that artists are becoming craftsmen, content to belabor the new materials with a sad lack of appreciation of theology, of scripture, of the sublime fittingness demanded by universal man in expressing the glory and love of God. Thus these craftsmen are content to experiment with anatomically grotesque statuary, with novelties of sculpture utilizing everything from tin cans to chicken wire. And because they have too hastily skimmed the principles of art in general, and the rich heritage of Christian art in particular, they can contribute little of permanence to a new concept of harmony between form and meaning.

There are some who think even now that this form of novelty and extreme "modernity" have already become obsolete. Only recently, Henry Hope Reed, Jr., associate professor of city planning at Yale, deplored the fixed ugliness in the "modernist" movement and expressed belief that it was time for architecture to replenish itself at the classical fountains.

The concern of many over "church art factories" and the modern iconography of sadly distorted statues is perhaps well founded, but there are bright prospects that this "phase" is a transitory one. In 1947, Pope Pius XII stated in his encyclical, *Mediator Deus:* "Modern pictures and statues, whose style is more adapted to the materials in use in the present day, are not to be condemned out of hand. On condition that these modern arts steer a middle course between an excessive realism on the one hand and an exaggerated symbolism on the other, and take into account more the needs of the Christian community than the personal taste and judgment of the artist, they should be allowed full scope if with due reverence and honor they put themselves at the service of our churches and sacred rites."

The Catholic bishops of the United States have been urged to set up "commissions on building and art" to control the new development. While few have deemed this necessary, it would be a wise precaution. Other church groups have maintained an attitude of restraint, establishing similar denominational governing commissions, not as a hindrance but as an aid to the development of a great church art in America.

The churches presented in this chapter are fine examples of artistic progression. We find some beautiful in an adapted manner, but we offer them without individual critical comment. They stand as a part of the record of the present, and in some degree, insofar as they contribute to the rounding out of the historic cycle, point to the future achievement which should be America's.

To some extent, the work of transition from old to new is being most worthily done in smaller chapels. Some of these are: the Chapel at the Massachusetts Institute of Technology, designed by Eero Saarinen and Associates; the Three

St. Michael's Chapel, St. Columbans, Nebraska
(A. E. Miller, Architect)
(Riley Engineering Industries, Fabricator & Erector, Hartford, Iowa)

Chapels (Catholic, Protestant, and Jewish) of the Interfaith Center of Brandeis University in Waltham, Massachusetts, designed by Harrison and Abramovitz; the Chapel at the Illinois Institute of Technology, designed by Ludwig Mies van der Rohe; the Chapel at Florida Southern College and the Wayfarers' Chapel, both designed by Frank Lloyd Wright; the multi-purpose chapel of the Air Force Academy, which has interpretative styling that suggests the folded wings of planes while giving the impression of flight; and the monastic St. John's Abbey, Collegeville, Minnesota, designed by Marcel Breuer.

In these are indications of forward development. Transition can even more clearly be seen in the unusual First Christian Church of Oklahoma City. Here is an almost complete break with tradition. Designed by R. Duane Conner for the Disciples of Christ, this church presents distinct innovations. The church, completed in 1955, consists of two buildings, a sanctuary and an educational building. Rising over these is a separate 150-foot bell tower, from the top of which flares a natural-gas torch. The church proper is constructed much like a hugh concrete eggshell, arching 110 feet. An escalator from the entrance foyer carries worshipers up to the sanctuary, which has a capacity of twenty-two hundred. The pulpit itself is raised and lowered on an elevator.

Before we give further consideration to the "new look" in church construction, a word is in order about an interesting, though minor, phase of church development in this country. This has to do with missionary activity in areas where large enough sums of money are not available for permanent construction, and where the potential success of the religious venture is uncertain. To fill the need for a house of worship under these conditions, prefabricated buildings have come into use. Their practicality and economy seem to assure that

they will enjoy increasing popularity in the years to come.

The most recent of these was put up on the grounds of the Columban Fathers' headquarters at St. Columban's, Nebraska, to test its effectiveness in the missions of the Far East, particularly Korea. This was a drastically new idea in church construction, a Geodesic dome made of plastic, aluminum, and plywood. The dome is built from the top down, with plywood sheets bolted around a center mast which is then raised by winch or pulley as additional sheets are bolted. The church has 1,200 feet of floor space, weighs 3,600 pounds and can withstand 100-mile-an-hour winds. The dome also has 125 stained glass windows in six different shapes; it can accommodate four hundred worshipers. Designed by Richard Buckminster Fuller, the prefabricated geodesic church comes in graduated larger sizes. Its adaptability, economy, strength, and the use of new materials make it a missionary innovation which is truly forward-looking, and considered the first of its type in the world.

A notable example of the transition from the old to the modern church building is the Christian Church of Columbus, Indiana. It was in 1937 that a block of land known as Railroad Square, or Commercial Park, was purchased, and plans made for putting up a new church. Only thirty years before its purchase this plot had been spread with cinders and used as a hitching lot for farmers' wagons. The commission for the church design was given to Eliel Saarinen, a world famous Finnish-American architect of Bloomfield Hills, Michigan. The architect and building committee decided in the beginning that, as the Disciples of Christ have never been led by human opinion and tradition, they should ignore tradition in planning the new structure, and make it fit the needs and promote the purposes of the Christians who were

Christian Church, Columbus, Indiana

to use it. They decided to make it as simple and fundamental as the gospel it proclaims.

The architect, speaking to the committee on building, declared: "The design of almost every other church that has been built during the present era is an imitation of Gothic or some other historical style. Our forefathers, fathers, and we ourselves have been using the dead styles of alien cultures. We have remodeled them to serve any purpose, no matter whether they were appropriate to that purpose or not. As your church has been based upon the fundamentals of Christianity, so the new architectural thought is endeavoring to build upon the fundamental principles of architecture."

The church was begun in 1940 and completed in May, 1942. The east portion contains the church proper and the chapel, where services attended by comparatively small audiences are held. Below these rooms is the auditorium for social gatherings and entertainments. In the bridge which connects the east and west wings are the church offices and activities room on the first floor, the choir and Sunday School classrooms above. In the west wing are the departmental rooms for beginners, primary, and junior grades, with the nursery school below the beginners' department and the rooms for the young people's classes and meetings below the primary room. It thus serves as a complete religious unit for their purposes.

The reflecting pool and the sunken garden give all the rooms on the lower floor, through full length windows, a pleasing, though not distracting, outlook. The tower, which is 166 feet high from the level of the reflecting pool, contains chimes and the bell of the old Tabernacle church. The tower and east wing are wired for sound, and organ music may be broadcast.

In the years since its dedication, hundreds of architects and students have visited the church, as have building committees,

*Boston Avenue Methodist Church, Tulsa, Oklahoma
(photo by Bob McCormack)*

and many of its features have been incorporated into new church buildings across the country. Thus, the congregation, architect, and building committee know that they have pioneered to some degree in the field of church architecture.

In recent years churches of Europe have been notable for innovations which at first, to the traditional-minded, seem startling. They have in most instances, however, shown authentic theological interpretation, and have used art in a most effective manner, subordinating the simple, stark form of their architecture to an inspirational quality in the interior appointments. Designed as a whole, with art amplifying the meaning of the overall design, they have achieved the ideal balance so necessary to fine church architecture; for the setting should be the primary concern in considering what is to be placed within, and liturgy and architecture have thus to come to a meeting of purpose in all proper development.

Tulsa, Oklahoma, has a church which exemplifies in its every detail the blending of modern design with religious validity. This is the Boston Avenue Methodist Church. The congregation had established itself by 1900 in what had been only a decade before an Indian village of a few hundred souls. The present church is the third in its history, and was completed in 1929. It is, by any standards, a splendid achievement.

The guiding hand behind what at the time seemed, and was, a formidable task was Dr. John A. Rice, the pastor who in 1925 named a building committee to see to it that a suitable church be provided for the growing congregation. Architects submitted designs, and one was contracted for; but the committee had acted in haste, and soon realized that the plan did not fit the concept of Dr. Rice, who "wanted to be free to build one church before which he could stand in

Boston Avenue Methodist Church, Tulsa, Oklahoma
(photo by Bob McCormack)

the rain and let it talk to him; he wanted an interior that would impel him to worship whether he wanted to or not."

The committee was dissatisfied. Then the chairman's wife thought of the Quaker and artist, Miss Adah Robinson. Miss Robinson submitted a plan—and the earlier architect's contract was canceled. A new contract was arranged between Miss Robinson, the firm of Rush, Endacott and Rush, engineers, and the committee.

Miss Robinson supervised all the art features, holding to her plan for a church which would be a whole creation in "spiritual.terms." Steel and concrete are its structural components. The plan is splendid, huge; it takes in a block measuring 218 by 225 feet on the longest and widest boulevard in the city, Boston Avenue. The church tower, situated in the center of the block, is 225 feet high. The building has no "rear"; each of its four sides has a front entrance, and all entrances are adorned with sculpted figures of historic or symbolic significance, such as The Wesley Group, The Circuit Rider Group, and groups representing Worship, Religious Education, and Human Service. The windows are a departure from church tradition in that they are transparent, the emphasis being on light rather than on color, and their effectiveness is achieved through leaded shapes and color, beveling, and symbolic shape. Light was given emphatic treatment in the church's design. Not only the windows, but shafts of glass set at angles to the four directions atop the tower, grillework in doors, windows, and decorative wood, skylights, and even symbolic motifs, were conceived as exponents of light. The principal motif is that of praying hands, used on the exterior, and some interior, finials (terminal points of apexes). The finials of the auditorium are an architectural treatment of the tritoma, a flower indigenous to Oklahoma; these finials are designed to catch the light at all hours of the day.

St. Columba's Church, St. Paul, Minnesota
(Warren Reynolds, infinity inc.)

Dr. Rice had from the beginning had his heart set on a community hall and social lobby. He was, moreover, vitally interested in the subject of education. The church has provided not only for his first wishes, but has among its 125 rooms a library, gymnasium, dining room, kitchens, and classrooms for beginners, young people, and adults. Its Sanctuary seats two thousand and its Community Hall twelve hundred. Above the first four floors which comprise the base of the building rise the eight floors of the tower, each of these floors measuring 20 feet by 28 feet, exclusive of elevator, hall, and stairway. The farsightedness of the church's designers is evident in that the church today accommodates thousands of worshipers and church school students, and facilities for their social and civic activities. The church has a combined choir of five hundred voices, all schooled in the fine points of church music.

The building cost one-and-a-half million dollars and its upkeep is costly. Yet no one knew better than Dr. Rice that fine appointments do not make a church. In speaking of the excellence of the building and art, he said, "All this cannot make a church. These wonders may increase all the more the futility of a hollow sham. Is it not to provide creative conditions for fulfilling the task Jesus gave to His disciples and, through them, to us—the task, namely, of bearing witness to Him? . . . Toward these deeper meanings of Jesus every stone, appointment, line, form, color, leads. In Him they all alike find their fulfilment."

There have, unfortunately, been estrangements between spirit and architecture in the past. Some Europeans, as well as Americans, have commissioned artists to produce church adornment which, because of the artists' lack of deep Christian appreciation, has been executed without religious content. Such art will almost inevitably appear out of place in

St. Columba's Church, St. Paul, Minnesota
(Warren Reynolds, infinity inc.)

a church, distracting the worshiper with its look of "not belonging." Art and architecture must harmonize, of course, but this achievement is not in itself enough if the finished work is to have religious meaning.

Another point of transition—and dispute—is the use of new materials. Flexibility in design and execution is easily achieved through the various uses of plastics, tiles, linoleum, Fiberglas, and other substances. It is hardly valid to say, as some do, that the modern churches are "not religious" because their appearance is so different from the traditional, or because they employ building materials not used, or known, in earlier times.

In two notable instances the eminent architect Barry Byrne of Chicago has blended an understanding of religious feeling with the potential flexibility of new materials and modern design. The first example of his achievement is the Roman Catholic church of St. Francis Xavier in Kansas City, Missouri.

Behind its plan is an early church symbol. The most familiar type of church design today, whether in basilica or Gothic pattern, is the cruciform, intended to commemorate the Sacrifice of Christ on the Cross. Just as familiar as the sign of the Cross in early Christian symbols, however, was the "ichthus," a fish in water with a basket of loaves on its back. This figure is one of the oldest symbols of Christ.

In designing St. Francis Xavier church, Mr. Byrne follows the line of the ichthus. This ancient theme thus finds new expression in our time, with the aid of modern material and methods of construction. The church is formed to resemble a "fish," which derives from the letters of the Greek word ἰχθύς which, as an acrostic, constitutes the first letters of the words: "Jesus Christ, God's Son, Savior."

The church design focuses on the high altar. This has been held to the beauty of simplicity, with the motif of the ichthus

*First Unitarian Society Church, Madison, Wisconsin
(William Wollin Studios)*

retained in the pedestal part of each altar. Back of the high altar, set atop a 14-foot pedestal of imperial black marble, is the heroic statue of Christ the High Priest, with arms outstretched to men. The side altars are recessed, each located in a semi-chapel.

Along the sides of the church, on the upper wall, are the fourteen Stations of the Cross, done in marble bas-relief with emphasis on the figure of Christ. Early Christian art has influenced their form. The choir is located at the end of the nave.

The church of St. Francis Xavier has a seating capacity of one thousand. Its dimensions are: length, 160 feet; width, 96 feet; height, 45 feet.

Besides the customary marble and wood (white oak in this instance) a variety of newer materials have been used in the church's interior. New adaptations are seen in window frames, radiant heating, glass entry, acoustical blocks, and recessed lighting.

Another design based on the "fish" form was executed by the same architect in St. Columba's Roman Catholic church of St. Paul, Minnesota. A unique church even in the area of contemporary architecture, St. Columba's has a spacious, unobstructed interior. To the design has been added an Irish round tower of buff Indiana limestone, matching the church exterior, topped with a stainless steel cross.

Thousands of people have visited these two churches and are impressed not only by the novelty of design, but by the modernity of its religious expression.

One of the most forward-looking architects of our time is Frank Lloyd Wright. A strong advocate of functional design, he has introduced many ideas which will contribute to the evolution of a definitive modern form. An unusual church

First Unitarian Society Church, Madison, Wisconsin
(William Wollin Studios)

design by Mr. Wright is the Meeting House of the First Unitarian Society of Madison, Wisconsin.

Commenting on the structure, the architect said: "As the square has always signified integrity and the sphere universality, the triangle stands for aspiration. . . . Here is a church where the whole edifice is in the attitude of prayer. Instead of excluding the outside prospect, which is beautiful, we have allowed it to come in facing the audience to become part of the background for music and preacher."

The minister, Max D. Gaebler, declared: "Inside the church, as one faces the prow, the powerful focus upon the pulpit and the strong vertical thrust of the prow create a feeling of unity and elevation which surpasses description. Yet when one faces the hearth room, there is by contrast a warm and intimate feeling which suggests the flux of daily life.

"The utter simplicity of the assembly room is friendly, not austere. The large, clear glass areas, the warm colors, the closeness of the congregation to the pulpit—all this helps to create an atmosphere of directness and honesty, with no barriers of false formalism interposed between minister and congregation. It would be difficult to speak or think anything but the truth in such a setting. Mr. Wright has caught the spirit of liberal religion and has given it architectural embodiment."

To the viewer, the dominant feature of this church is the up-thrust triangle of the roof, which, while prow-like in appearance, is vestigially a steeple and yet part of the church proper. Two ridges converge to form the prow, while the roof is supported by a series of trusses. The interior has an interesting appearance, particularly in that its ceiling has a "warped," yet elevating, look. As the prow continues forward, exteriorly it is cantilevered out beyond the sidewalls and the piers of the rostrum within. The trusses also extend outward, forming a sloping overhang at the sides.

Blending into a unity of site and building, a distinctive

Central Lutheran Church, Portland, Oregon

mark of Wright's planning, the church is both functional and symbolic. A functional innovation is that the pews, which face toward the prow and pulpit, are movable and can be turned in the opposite direction, toward the hearth room, for use during concerts, movies, and such. The pews can also be moved to the side so that the area can be used for dancing and socials in a "living-room" manner. When the gatherings are smaller, the pulpit end and the hearth end of the church can be divided by draperies of red, purple, and copper green. These draperies were designed by the architect's wife and executed by the women of the congregation. With the materials used, including flax, rayon, banana rope, sisal, and metal ribbon, the draperies effectively gather the colors of indoors and out.

This modern church, designed by one of America's most noted architects, followed a historic practice in its building. The stone was brought from a nearby quarry, and the members of the congregation worked as volunteers, contributing greatly to its satisfactory completion.

Response to the unusual design has been spontaneous and favorable. The numerous visitors are not idly curious but genuinely intrigued by this modern church structure.

The architect Pietro Belluschi has long been recognized as one of the outstanding exponents of modern ideas in church structure. The designer of numerous churches, Mr. Belluschi has consistently brought out innovations in design, giving to contemporary religious structures some of their most outstanding features. This is true of the Central Lutheran Church in Portland, Oregon, which he designed and in which he has made an adaptation of the Gothic. Here he has worked with three elements of the Gothic spirit: the pointed arch, subdued and brought into new harmony; the vertical line which here is multiplied; and the introduction of light which

Central Lutheran Church, Portland, Oregon

increases in brilliance as it reaches the chancel. In his own words, he has here presented "a more human scale . . . so as to produce the kind of atmosphere most conducive to worship."

In the design of Central Lutheran Church laminated wood arches were called for. These span forty-four feet across the nave and support the roof, at the same time giving an exposed beam effect which in itself helps to draw attention toward the altar. At the chancel end there is a semicircular shell of concrete with a patterned brick veneer on its outside surface and acoustic plaster on its inner wall, which is painted a pale blue.

Behind the altar and on the back curved wall of the chancel is a wood screen of geometric pattern, in which the central motif of a cross is discernible, but not so outstanding as to be obtrusive. This serves also as the organ screen. This motif is repeated on the side walls of the nave.

On the street side of the church, to one's left facing the altar, the wooden verticals serve as the mullions of a continuous screen of glass. The glass is not stained in the usual sense, but an imported English glass in many colors is used—both as an economy and as a source of soft light throughout the nave. By the arrangement of small panes in graduated shadings ranging from pale bluish gray through blue and violet to brilliant red, and by staining the wood of the opposite wall a "natural" color and the arches a Venetian red with deep blue on the purlins, the nave is flooded with a rich "royal purple."

With the half circle of the chancel curving wider than the width of the nave and taller than the roof of the nave, a means of introducing a focused brightness into the chancel was achieved. The light comes through a clerestory and the offset sides of the chancel shell. These areas are fitted with amber panes of glass, and light is directed onto the chancel shell without the source of light being visible to the congregation.

Los Angeles Temple, Los Angeles, California
(courtesy D. W. Evans and Associates)

The light to the sides of the chancel can be regulated by venetian blinds.

Flanking the church is a complete Sunday School facility, while in the basement there are meeting rooms, a kitchen, and a recreation area for parish social functions.

Rising at the corner is a free-standing, square, open steeple surmounted by a beamed wooden cross. The steeple is wooden, and has an airy grace.

While there were economic limitations on the construction of this church and facilities, its design and modern simplicity make it noteworthy. The building seats one thousand, and serves to center the various activities of the group in one building. With its extreme severity of line, it illustrates a thoughtful trend toward the development of an indigenous style of church architecture.

We have seen exemplified in the Mormon churches considered earlier the type of structure which was erected during the immediate post-missionary years. The need of this group for facilities is a growing one, and here, too, progress is evident in the fields of construction and design.

The Los Angeles Temple is one of the most impressive of the new Latter-day Saints structures. Designed by Edward O. Anderson, it is located on a prominent hill near Westwood Village in Los Angeles, California. It can be seen from such distant points as San Pedro and Catalina Island, and from ships twenty-five miles at sea.

Named "Building of the Year" in Los Angeles in 1954, the Temple is 364 feet wide and 241 deep, and measures 190,614 square feet in floor space. The high tower rises 152 feet above the roof. Upon it stands the figure of the angel Moroni. (The Mormon faith is based on the visitation of the angel to Joseph Smith, founder, in 1823.) The building exterior is faced with sparkling Mo-sai, a cast stone of quartz and other aggregates.

Los Angeles Temple, Los Angeles, California
(courtesy D. W. Evans and Associates)

Stone grilles over the windows add to the beauty of the whole.

Inside the Temple are ninety rooms, many of them with a capacity of three hundred persons. The chapel in the southwest wing seats three hundred and eighty. All materials used were selected to withstand wear and keep maintenance costs low. Eight types of marble, quarried throughout the world, adorn the interior. Tile and costly carpets cover the floors. Vinylized fabric and mosaics cover many of the walls. In the ordinance rooms wall murals are brilliantly executed and offer startling effects in their decorative detail.

The statue on the tower is of cast aluminum covered with gold leaf, and was executed by Millard F. Malin.

The Mormons have adopted a similar style of building for their temples in the Hawaiian Islands.

While it may have been appropriate to include the following cathedral in the chapter devoted to Cathedrals and Temples, it was reserved for this chapter because its modern aspect is its special distinction.

The Roman Catholic Cathedral of the Sacred Heart of Salina, Kansas, stands in the great wheat-growing area of the world. Moving across the state, the traveler sees an endless succession of huge grain elevators rising from the landscape. The Cathedral, which is located in the center of downtown Salina, was planned to reflect its surroundings, and by contemporary design to fit in with the familiar building pattern of the territory. It was therefore decided to use the grain elevator as the motif in the Cathedral's architectural design.

The architect was Edward J. Schulte of Cincinnati, Ohio. The plan is a simple rectangle, fronted by a one-story narthex to accommodate the entrance. The narthex is accented by a crucifix and a processional panel of sculpture.

Forward from the nave is the sanctuary and the main altar, behind which is a semi-circular choir loft. The wall behind

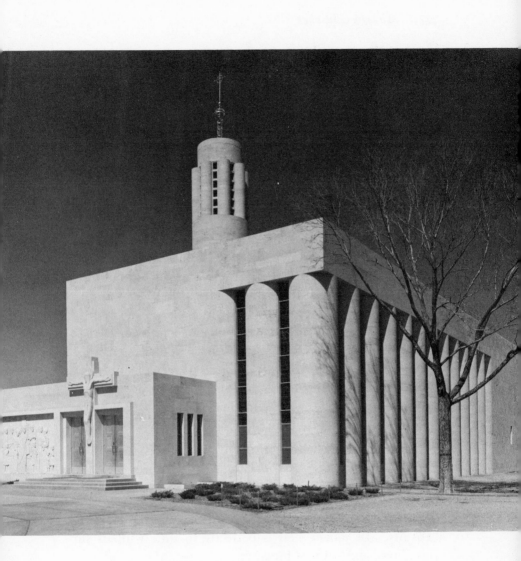

Sacred Heart Cathedral, Salina, Kansas
(Edward J. Schulte, Architect)

the choir is executed in a simple abstract pattern of gold and black mosaic. Suspended from the tester over the altar is a large crucifix, the cross of blackest ebony and the corpus of ivory.

Flanking the rear curve of the back wall of the sanctuary there are six tall bas-relief figures of saints, three to a side, one above the other in columnar fashion.

Edging the side aisle, halfway down the left side of the nave, is the baptistry. This forms the base of the round tower which rises aloft like an elevator, dominating the series of circular forms that make up the outer wall in a repetitive line. Between the baptistry and the sanctuary there is a transept chapel called the Lady Chapel. This features an altar of black marble and a figure of the Assumption of the Blessed Mother carved in stone and covered with gold leaf.

Opposite the baptistry is a row of long stained glass windows which colorfully carry out the motif. The flat ceiling of the church is decorated in a geometric pattern derived from the designs of the plains Indians. The church seats nine hundred people, and the choir accommodates an additional sixty.

The entire structure is faced with a beautiful stone, found in a quarry about forty miles away. This stone has a shell-like structure, resembling somewhat the qualities of imported travestine stone.

While the Cathedral of the Sacred Heart is distinctly contemporary in its overall aspect, it cannot be said to represent "novelty." Its modernness is perfectly in tune with its surroundings, and with its function.

Church building in the United States, starting with missions of Spanish design and continuing through the prerevolutionary days, when those who sought freedom of worship raised the first colonial structures, through the missionary era of 1800 to 1860 and the contemporary movement, looks

Sacred Heart Cathedral, Salina, Kansas
(Edward J. Schulte, Architect)

to a promising future. In all these years, the contribution of churches to political and social development was immense.

Some European thinkers have charged that churches and church art in the United States are "conservative"—that the dominance of the Anglo-Saxon spirit and the intermingling of nationalities have had a deterrent effect upon the development of a unique church style. Others have thought that church development is retarded by our lack of state grants or endowments, or that our emphasis on the technological has hampered expression.

We must acknowledge that church building in the United States only began to come into its own after the close of the Civil War, and that many of the churches built at that time were works of haste, repeatedly enlarged to accommodate an ever-growing membership. Our haste, still much in evidence today, has led to some ineptness and confusion, it is true, but a time of closer harmony between architects and artists is coming, a time of the unified accomplishment that makes for great churches.

It is perhaps not yet time to say that this future is assured. Certain cautions will be necessary. The objective should be to endow the church edifice with the utmost expressiveness, so that it may even more effectively hold its place among the social and spiritual ties that bind mankind together. The church should be a concrete expression of the spiritual awareness that makes men considerate and understanding of each other. This, some will say, is the function of religious teaching and practice. True, but this function requires churches where faith may be taught and practiced. Even the United Nations building, with all its council rooms, found it essential to provide a "place" for prayer and meditation.

Churches are outward expressions of the relationship of God to the soul of man. If we forget this we will raise unworthy churches which will neither serve man in the present, reflect his history, nor enrich the future. Only if in building upon the past we progress toward our highest goal, will we be able to say with the Psalmist: "I have built a House for Thy dwelling, to be Thy most firm Throne forever."

APPENDIX

This listing of churches, temples, cathedrals, and synagogues is arranged according to state. It includes thumbnail sketches of buildings covered in greater detail in text, as well as many which, chiefly because of space limitations, could not be given fuller treatment.

In each instance when they are known, we include the unique attributes of the churches named. We also designate the denomination of each, except in a few cases where the information was not supplied.

While the list is far from exhaustive, it is a careful rendering of the houses of worship cited, in response to our inquiries, by state and denominational historic societies, historians, chancery offices, architects, and architectural journals. It is intended as a guide to the traveler, whether his vehicle be mobile or as stationary as an armchair.

ALABAMA

St. John's Episcopal Church, Montgomery. 1837; present church 1854. Jefferson Davis worshiped here when Montgomery was the state capital in the early days of the Civil War.

Ascension Church, Montgomery. Episcopal. Hailed as probably the outstanding example of Gothic architecture in the South, this church was designed by Ralph Adams Cram.

Christ Church, Mobile. Episcopal. 1822; present church 1840. The first Protestant church in Alabama. Nearly destroyed by two hurricanes in nine years, this church has lost its steeple, but is still a classic beauty.

Cathedral of the Immaculate Conception, Mobile. Catholic. 1835. An old church whose towers were landmarks for seafarers of the Gulf. In recent remodeling this cathedral has been given one of the finest sets of stained glass windows in the South.

First Presbyterian, Birmingham. c. 1871. The first church to be erected in Birmingham after the city's incorporation. Noteworthy stained glass windows in symbolic classical design.

St. Andrew's, Prairieville. Episcopal. 1854. A distinctive and picturesque rural church, erected entirely by slave labor.

St. Mary's Catholic Church, Mobile. 1867. Its second pastor was the priest-poet, Father Abram J. Ryan, "the poet of the Confederacy."

ARIZONA

San Xavier Del Bac, on Papago Indian Reservation, ten miles s.w. of Tucson. Catholic. 1792. Built near the original site of Kino church, now destroyed. The Indians call this Franciscan Mission "La Paloma Blanca del Desierto" (White Dove of the Desert).

Mormon Temple, Mesa. 1927. One of the few Mormon temples in the South; first in Arizona.

St. Paul's, Tombstone. Episcopal. 1882. First Episcopal church in the state. Endicott Peabody was its first pastor.

Chapel of the Holy Cross, Sedonia. Christian. 1956. One of two churches receiving top awards in the American Institute of Architects competition, this church sits in a mountain cleft and is fronted by a huge cross. Designed by Aushen and Allen of San Francisco.

ARKANSAS

First Congregational Church, Little Rock. 1881.
Christ Church, Little Rock. Episcopal. 1839. The first Episcopal church
in the state.

CALIFORNIA

First Unitarian Church, San Francisco. 1850; present church 1889. In
the churchyard is the tomb of the Reverend Thomas Starr King, one
of the two Californians in the Hall of Fame, Washington, D.C.
St. Joseph's, Sawyer's Bar. Catholic. The first church in northern California, noted for a remarkable painting of the Crucifixion which was
transported around Cape Horn from Austria.
California Missions. (See Chapter II, on Missions, for complete list.)
St. Albert, Compton. Catholic. Recent. A fine example of modern architecture with tall campanile, designed by Chaix and Johnson.
First Presbyterian Church, San Francisco. 1849.
Trinity Church, San Francisco. Episcopal. 1849. First Episcopal church
in the state.
First Church, Berkeley. Congregational. c. 1860. One of the first Protes-
tant churches on the Pacific coast.
Church of the Nativity, El Monte. 1956. A prize-winning design for a
modern church. Chaix and Johnson, architects.
Corpus Christi Church, San Francisco. Catholic. 1950's. A modern church
showing transition toward American architecture. Mario J. Ciampi,
architect.
Los Angeles Temple, Los Angeles. Mormon. 1954. An impressive modern
building, named "Building of the Year" in Los Angeles in 1954.
Old St. Mary's, San Francisco. Catholic. 1854. California's first cathedral;
no longer diocesan cathedral. Survived earthquake and the ensuing
fire of 1906.

COLORADO

Our Lady of Guadalupe, Conejos. Catholic. 1855. The oldest Catholic
church in the state; rebuilt in 1926 and 1948.

Sheldon Jackson Memorial Church, Fairplay. Community-Protestant. 1874. This church is dedicated to the memory of an outstanding pioneer preacher known as the "Bishop of All Beyond." Sheldon Jackson traveled by horse and stage, and founded many churches in the West before 1877.

Georgetown Episcopal Church, Georgetown. 1867. This early church has a bell tower rising from the ground, an innovation in its day.

St. James', Central City. Methodist. 1859; present building 1872. Church begun by the first lay preacher of the Methodists in this territory.

St. John's-in-the-Wilderness, Denver. Episcopal cathedral. 1862. The first Episcopal church in the state.

St. Mary's, Central City. Catholic. 1893. An ancient mining town church.

St. Mary's, Leadville. Catholic. 1888. Early mining town church.

Temple Emmanuel, Denver. 1874. An early western synagogue.

CONNECTICUT

Congregational Church, Old Lyme. 1816. The fifth, and present, church, built in 1907–10, is a replica of the fourth church, and is described as "one of the most perfect early nineteenth century churches of New England."

Center Church on the Green, New Haven. Puritan. 1812–14. An old meeting house which contributed much to architectural interest in the "colonial style." Its membership can be traced back to 1637.

United Church on the Green, New Haven. 1813. Here in 1855 Henry Ward Beecher preached opposition to slavery and support of the John Brown movement. Noted colonial architecture.

Center Congregational Church, Hartford. 1807. The oldest church organized in the state, it marked a turning-point away from colonial New England architecture.

Congregational Church, Farmington. 1771. Early colonial architecture.

Congregational Church, Litchfield. 1828. Restored colonial church with distinctive features of barrel-vaulting.

Old Trinity Church, Brooklyn. Congregational. 1771. Colonial church of hand-hewn logs.

Immaculate Conception, Waterbury. Catholic. c. 1928. Fine traditional architecture.

Christ Church, Stratford. Episcopal. 1707. The first Episcopal church in the state.

First Church, Hartford. Congregational. 1632. One of the great historical pioneer churches; pure colonial architecture.

First Presbyterian Church, Stamford. 1958. Modern church designed in form of fish, with Gothic-style supports and stained glass ascending to the apex of roof.

DELAWARE

Trinity Church ("Old Swedes' Church"), now in Wilmington. Swedish-Lutheran. Founded 1638. Originally Episcopal; claimed to be the oldest Protestant church in North America still in active use as a place of worship.

Christ Episcopal Church, near Laurel. 1771. This church is noted for its original interior woodwork.

Immanuel Episcopal Church, New Castle. 1703. One of the earliest congregations here; organized in 1689.

Barratt's Chapel, Frederica. Methodist. 1780. Called the "Cradle of Methodism in America," the first sacrament was given here in 1784.

Christ Episcopal Church, Dover. 1734. Parish church and burial place of Caesar Rodney, signer of the Declaration of Independence. Parish established in 1705.

Old Drawyers Presbyterian Church, Odessa. Present building 1773. Colonial meeting house.

St. Francis Xavier, near Middletown. Catholic. 1704. Original site chosen by the Jesuits for the college which later became Georgetown University.

DISTRICT OF COLUMBIA

Islamic Center, Washington. Dedicated 1958. This sect's cultural and religious center in the United States.

St. Patrick's, Washington. Catholic. 1790. Edward Hoban, architect of the White House, insisted that this church be built to serve the Irish workers on the government buildings. The oldest church of any faith in the national capital.

Holy Trinity, Georgetown. Catholic. 1784. Church begun with the founding of Georgetown University.

Washington Cathedral (Cathedral of St. Peter and St. Paul). Episcopal. Cornerstone laid 1907; building now more than sixty percent completed. This will be the sixth largest cathedral in the world; five denominations now worship here regularly.

St. John's, Forest Glen. Catholic. 1775. The church of Father John Carroll before he became the first bishop of the United States.

St. Paul's, Rock Creek Parish. Episcopal. 1726. Earliest Episcopal church in the vicinity of the future Capitol.

Shrine of the Immaculate Conception, Washington. Catholic. Begun in 1920; to be completed. The national shrine of the Roman Catholics of the United States.

FLORIDA

Mission of Nombre de Dios and Shrine of Nuestra Señora de la Leche y Buen Parto, U.S. Highway 1, St. Augustine. Catholic. 1567; present chapel 1915. This is the site of the first Mass celebrated on the North American continent; the oldest permanent mission: 1567–1763.

Trinity Church, St. Augustine. Episcopal. 1764. Formerly St. Peter's; the first Episcopal church in the state.

Cathedral of St. Augustine. Catholic. 1791. The oldest Catholic parish north of Mexico, the Cathedral's parish records date back to 1597.

St. Andrew's, Jacksonville. Episcopal. 1888. A memorial church to Bishop Young.

GEORGIA

Christ Church, Savannah. Episcopal. 1733. The first Episcopal church in the state.

St. Luke's Cathedral, Atlanta. Episcopal. 1882. Originally founded as St. Stephen's during the last year of the Civil War, it was supported by many high-ranking Confederate officers, notably General Polk.

Immaculate Conception, Atlanta. Catholic. 1848; present building 1873. The courage of its pastor saved the City Hall, Court House, and four churches from destruction by Sherman's Army.

Redeemer Lutheran, Atlanta. 1903. A notable example of modified Gothic architecture.

IDAHO

Cataldo Mission, at Cataldo, 20 miles east of Coeur d'Alene. Catholic. 1846. Building erected by Indian labor; oldest Catholic mission church in the territory.

Christ Church, Boise. Episcopal. 1866. Formerly called St. Michael's, this was the first church built in Boise in the frontier days.

St. John's Cathedral, Boise. Catholic. 1906. A western use of Romanesque design blended with twelfth century Gothic.

Temple of Idaho Falls. Mormon. 1945. Its foundation rests on volcanic lava bedrock; structure is reinforced concrete.

ILLINOIS

Holy Family, at Cahokia, East St. Louis. Catholic. 1699; present church 1799. Probably the oldest church in the Mississippi valley; now being preserved as historic site.

Immaculate Conception, Kaskaskia. Catholic. Present church 1893. Called the "Shrine of the Liberty Bell of the West" because of the bell which arrived from France in 1743.

St. Peter's Cathedral, Belleville. Catholic. 1866. Outstanding example of English Gothic architecture.

St. Joseph, Prairie du Roche. Catholic. 1858. As a mission church this was endowed with a gift of precious vessels donated by Louis XIV of France.

First Presbyterian Church, Springfield. 1828. The present church, built in 1890, acquired the original church's Lincoln Pew in 1912.

St. Anne, at St. Anne. Catholic. 1873. The present church, built in 1911, is the place of the original shrine of the saint in Illinois.

St. John L'Erable, Ashkum. Catholic. 1874. This was called the "Wooden Cathedral" of the Midwest.

Trinity Church, Chicago. Episcopal. 1844; present church 1886. This church was burned out during the great Chicago fire of 1871.

Bahai House of Worship, Wilmette. 1920; dedicated 1953. Open to all people for prayer and meditation.

St. John's, Albion. Episcopal. 1825. The first Episcopal church in the state.

St. Peter's Church, Chicago. Catholic. 1952. Modern downtown "Loop" church.

Trinity Lutheran Church, Rockford. 1895. A notable example of modern colonial architecture.

First St. Paul's, Chicago. Lutheran. 1846; present church 1910. The founding church for more than twenty-four Lutheran churches in the area.

First Methodist Church (Chicago Temple), Chicago. Dedicated 1924. Tallest building in the "Loop," this church has its chapel on top, sanctuary on the ground floor.

INDIANA

St. Francis Xavier, Vincennes. Catholic. Present building 1826. Named the cathedral of the diocese of Vincennes in 1841. Like the town, however, the parish and the first church date back to the years of the Jesuit missionaries, who built the first mission there between 1733 and 1749.

St. Paul, New Alsace. Catholic. 1838. This church, originally built of logs in 1833, is the only church extant dedicated by the first bishop, Simon Brute.

St. Paul's, New Albany. Episcopal. 1834. The first Episcopal church in the state.

St. Michael, Madison. Catholic. 1839. The present building was constructed by the noted missionary, the Reverend Michael Shawe.

Little Cedar Grove Baptist Church, two miles east of Brookville. 1812. The oldest church building of the territory still on original site.

Christian Church, Columbus. Disciples of Christ. 1942. This church is distinctively modern, covers a city block.

IOWA

Congregational Church of Bradford ("Little Brown Church in the Vale"), Nashua. Organized 1855; erected 1860. Picturesque church, celebrated in the famous song, "The Church in the Wildwood."

St. Raphael Cathedral, Dubuque. Catholic. 1861. Noted cathedral along the Mississippi, it has paintings by Gregori of Florence, Italy.

Amana Colony Church, Amana. Church of the first settlers in the territory.

Cathedral of the Epiphany, Sioux City. Catholic. First church 1862; present 1891. A church historically associated with Father Pierre-Jean De Smet, Jesuit missionary.

Corpus Christi, Fort Dodge. Catholic. First church 1857; present 1883. Mother-church of northwestern Iowa.

Trinity Church, Muscatine. Episcopal. 1839. The first Episcopal church in the state.

Basilica of St. Francis Xavier, Dyersville. Catholic. 1888. One of the few Minor Basilicas in the United States.

St. John's Lutheran, Des Moines. 1865. Home church of the largest congregation of the United Lutheran Church of America.

KANSAS

First Church of Christ, Wabaunsee. Congregational. 1857; present church 1862. Known as the "Beecher Bible and Rifle Church"; founded by a colony which had emigrated from Connecticut to establish an anti-slavery movement in Kansas.

St. Fidelis, Victoria. Catholic. 1876; present church 1907. Known as the "Cathedral of the Plains," this church was built by the parishioners.

Bethany Evangelical Lutheran Church, Lindsborg. 1868; present church 1874. Scene of the first Messiah Festival sung there in 1882, and repeated each Easter. Noted paintings.

Cathedral of the Sacred Heart, Salina. Catholic. 1951. An outstanding example of modern architecture, and, with its grain-elevator motif, singularly adapted to the countryside it overlooks.

St. Francis, at St. Paul. Catholic. 1846. First mission church of the Jesuits to the Osage Indians.

St. Paul's, Leavenworth. Episcopal. 1856. The first Episcopal church in the state.

Sacred Heart Cathedral, Dodge City. Catholic. 1920. Notable Spanish architecture.

Old Cathedral of the Immaculate Conception, Leavenworth. Catholic. Early 1800's. This church erected by Bishop Miege served the Indian territory, and is both beautiful and historic.

KENTUCKY

St. Joseph, procathedral, Bardstown. Catholic. 1819. The first cathedral built west of the Allegheny Mountains; famed for the religious paintings it houses.

St. Thomas, Bardstown. Catholic. 1810. Used as a cathedral for nine years by the first bishop of the territory, B. J. Flaget.

Christ Church, Lexington. Episcopal. 1792. The first Episcopal church in the state.

Cathedral of the Assumption, Louisville. Catholic. 1849. An example of early American Gothic architecture.

Old Mulkey Meeting House, Tompkinsville. 1804. Log construction; associated with early pioneers and the family of Daniel Boone.

Cathedral Basilica of the Assumption, Covington. Catholic. 1901. Outstanding example of classic architecture; famed for its stained glass and sculptures.

Mud Meeting House, Harrodsburg. Dutch Reformed. 1800. Early mission church.

St. Francis Mission Church, White Sulphur. Catholic. Original building 1794; present church 1820. One of the first mission churches of eastern Kentucky.

Cane Ridge Meeting-house, Paris. Christian. 1791. The present church of the Christian denomination in Kentucky; being preserved as a memorial.

LOUISIANA

Trinity Church, New Orleans. Episcopal. Founded 1847; erected 1852. Noted for its stained glass windows.

St. Louis Cathedral, New Orleans. Catholic. 1718. One of the oldest churches in the state.

Immaculate Conception, Natchitoches. Catholic. Founded 1729; present church 1856. Romanesque architecture.

St. Augustine, Isle Brevelle. Catholic. 1856. Church built on the historic Cane River.

Christ Church, New Orleans. Episcopal. 1805. Cathedral and first Episcopal church in the state.

St. John's Cathedral, Lafayette. Catholic. 1919. Diocesan cathedral and the burial place of Bishop Jeanmard.

St. Martin's, St. Martinville. Catholic. 1757. The church of Evangeline and the Arcadians, of whom Longfellow wrote.

St. James Major, New Orleans. Catholic. 1954. Outstanding modern design.

MAINE

Trinity Church, Saco. Episcopal. 1636. The first Episcopal church in the state.

First Parish Church, Portland. Formerly Congregational, now Unitarian. 1718; third church erected 1825. The first church founded in Portland.

First Parish Church, Kennebunk. Now Unitarian. 1773. An outstanding colonial church building, its tower houses a Paul Revere bell.

St. Patrick's Church, Damariscotta Mills. Catholic. Founded 1796; erected 1803. The oldest Catholic church on the Atlantic seaboard, except for St. Augustine's, Florida. Paul Revere bell.

First Parish Church, Castine. Unitarian. 1790. Has a Bulfinch steeple and Paul Revere bell.

St. Denis, North Whitefield. Catholic. 1818. Early mission center of central Maine.

Immaculate Conception Cathedral, Portland. Catholic. 1869. Noted for its marble sanctuary and appointments.

Congregational Church, Harpswell. 1843. Built for the Reverend Elijah Kellogg.

Congregational Church, Kennebunk Port. 1764. Its beautiful portico and spire are in the best tradition of colonial design.

Old Alna Meetinghouse, Alna. 1789. Colonial design.

MARYLAND

Cathedral-Basilica of the Assumption of the Blessed Virgin Mary, Baltimore. Catholic. 1807. The mother-cathedral of American Catholicism; designed by Benjamin Latrobe. Houses the crypt of Bishop John Carroll, the first American Catholic Bishop and the brother of Charles Carroll, signer of the Declaration of Independence; also the crypt of Cardinal Gibbons. This church declared a basilica by Pope Pius XI.

St. John's, Forest Glen. Catholic. 1750. The first church of the Reverend (later first bishop) John Carroll, this building was erected on the Carroll estate.

St. Paul's, Baltimore. Episcopal. 1692; present structure 1856. The oldest Episcopal church in Baltimore.

Graceham Moravian Church, near Thurmont. 1822. Early colonial church of architectural significance.

Trinity Church, St. Mary's County. Episcopal. 1642. The first Episcopal church in the state.

Rehoboth Presbyterian Church, Rehoboth. c. 1725. One of the oldest churches of the denomination in the country.

St. Ignatius Church, St. Inigoes. Catholic. 1634; present church 1788. First Catholic mission in British North America.

MASSACHUSETTS

Christ Church ("The Old North Church"), Boston. Puritan-Episcopal. 1723. The church from whose steeple the signal lanterns were hung for Paul Revere.

The Old South Church, Boston. Puritan Meeting House. 1729. Built by Joshua Blanchard, this is a historic meeting house of the revolutionary forces.

First Church in Boston, Unitarian. 1630. Present (fifth) building 1867. Founded by John Winthrop. Its original Communion Silver can be seen at the Museum of Fine Arts, Boston.

The Park Street Church, Boston. Unitarian. 1809. Of Christopher Wren-type design.

King's Chapel, Boston. Now Unitarian. 1688; present church 1749. Designed by Peter Harrison. The first Anglican church in America, it was the "church of loyalty" to the king, and its roster was made up of leading citizens.

St. Paul's Cathedral, Boston. Episcopal. 1819. The "home" church of Daniel Webster; noted as the church which contributed most to the establishment of the Episcopal denomination.

Cathedral of the Holy Cross, Boston. Catholic. First church 1768. The see church of the Archbishop of Boston. Church of the famous bishop, Jean-Louis Lefebvre de Cheverus.

First Church in Roxbury. Unitarian. 1804. This church is known as the church of John Eliot, called the "Apostle to the Indians."

Temple Adath Israel, Boston. 1854. A synagogue noteworthy for its social and charitable work.

First Church of Christ, Scientist, Boston. Chartered 1879; built in 1894; extended in 1904. This is the mother-church of the Christian Science faith, founded by Mrs. Mary Baker Eddy.

The Arlington Street Church, Boston. Unitarian. The church associated with William Ellery Channing.

Christ Church, Cambridge. Episcopal. 1761. A church designed by Peter Harrison; associated with the early days of the American Revolution.

First Parish Meeting House, commonly called the "Old Ship," Hingham. Puritan. 1681. The oldest church building in New England, and one of the oldest in the country in continual use, this is an outstanding example of primitive colonial architecture.

Eliot Church, South Natick. Now Unitarian. 1828. One of the most charming of the small meeting houses, this is the fifth church built here. The first, called "The First Indian Church," was erected in 1651.

Unitarian Church, Wayland. 1815. Early colonial church.

Baptist Church, Framingham Center. 1825. One of the most interesting meeting houses of the period.

Church of the First Parish, Lancaster. Now Unitarian. 1816. The fifth church on this site, this has been called Bulfinch's masterpiece. It has a Paul Revere bell.

First Parish Meeting House, Groton. Unitarian. 1755. Rebuilt several times, this is one of the first and most picturesque of New England churches. It has a Paul Revere bell.

St. Michael's Cathedral, Springfield. Catholic. 1861. The first church of New England to be consecrated, it is noted for its stained glass windows.

Blessed Sacrament, Holyoke. Catholic. 1953. A unique structure, outstanding "church in the round."

Cathedral of St. Mary of the Assumption, Fall River. Catholic. 1852. Excellent architecture and stained glass windows.

Notre Dame de Lourdes, Fall River. Catholic. Has famous ceiling paintings by Ludovico Cremonini.

Christ Church, Quincy. Episcopal. 1689. Oldest continuous Episcopal church in the state.

MICHIGAN

Holy Redeemer, Eagle Harbor. Catholic. 1852. The oldest existing church built by Bishop Frederic Baraga, this is a remarkably fine example of braced frame construction.

Mariners' Church, Detroit. Episcopal. 1849. Honored as one of the few surviving structures of early Detroit, this church, originally built on the Detroit River, served transient fishermen on the Great Lakes. In 1955 it was moved to Woodbridge and Randolph Streets to become a part of Detroit's east side civic center.

Old Mission Church, Mackinac Island. Non-denominational. 1829. This church was built through the efforts of the Reverend W. W. Ferry, who founded an Indian Mission on the Island; Henry Schoolcraft, a pioneer of the state, was one of the church's leaders.

St. Peter's Cathedral, Marquette. Catholic. The tomb of Bishop Frederic Baraga is here.

St. Anne's Church, Mackinac Island. Catholic. c. 1840. Mission church still in use.

St. Andrew's Cathedral, Grand Rapids. Catholic. Founded 1833; present church 1849; rebuilt in 1903. Historic church of the Grand River.

St. Lorenz, Frankenmuth. Lutheran. 1845; present church 1880. Of great historical interest to the Lutheran church, Missouri Synod.

Holy Name of Mary Church, Sault Ste. Marie. Catholic. 1834; present church 1881. Outgrowth of Jesuit mission to Indians in 1641.

St. Paul's, Detroit. Episcopal. 1824. Cathedral; the first Episcopal church in the state.

MINNESOTA

St. Mary's, Warroad. Catholic. Memorial Church of Father Aulneau; present church 1952. A large all-weather log church, with locally split shakes on the roof. This church commemorates a missionary to the territory in 1734 who served at Fort St. Charles.

Church of the Ascension, Stillwater. Episcopal. 1846. The first Episcopal church in the state.

Holy Rosary, Grand Portage. Catholic. 1865. The oldest church in northeast Minnesota. Originally built of logs, now rebuilt, and still serving the Indian reservation.

Cathedral of St. Paul, in St. Paul. Catholic. 1841; present (fourth) building 1905–15. One of the largest and most beautiful cathedrals in the United States.

St. Columba's Roman Catholic Church, St. Paul. Recent. Example of modern architecture; based on the form of a fish, early symbol for Christ.

St. Peter's, Mendota. Catholic. 1855. The oldest Catholic structure in the state.

MISSISSIPPI

Church of the Redeemer, Biloxi. Episcopal. 1858; present building 1891. Church where Jefferson Davis worshiped.

St. Mary's Cathedral, Natchez. Catholic. 1841. The see church of the diocese of Natchez; also associated with the early missions of the area.

Christ Church, Church Hill. Episcopal. Founded 1820; built 1828. First Episcopal church in the state.

Clear Creek Church, Washington. Baptist. Early 1800's. Claimed to be the oldest Baptist church in Mississippi; built along the historic Natchez Trace.

The First Presbyterian Church, Port Gibson. 1807; present church 1859. Known as the "Church with the Hand Pointing Heavenward," because of its unique steeple.

MISSOURI

Old Cathedral of St. Louis. Catholic. 1770; present building 1831–34. Named for Louis IX of France, this is the first cathedral built west of the Mississippi.

Cathedral of St. Louis. Catholic. 1907–14. "New" cathedral of the archdiocese of St. Louis, this building has the greatest array of mosaics in the modern world.

St. Anne's, Normandy. Catholic. 1950. Noted for its stained glass.

Christ Church Cathedral, St. Louis. Episcopal. First church 1819; present 1859. This church is known for its Gothic-Revival interior and the carved reredos of Caen stone.

Christ Church, Boonville. Episcopal. 1840. Church erected in 1846. The oldest surviving Episcopal church west of the Mississippi.

Christ Church, Lexington. Episcopal. 1848. Noted for its interior of black walnut and its famous "painted glass" windows.

Church of St. Ferdinand, Florissant. Catholic. 1788; present building 1821. Noted for its paintings imported from Europe.

Grace Presbyterian Church, Crystal City. 1895. English glassmakers here were the prime movers behind this church. It is ivy-covered; located on an entire block of beautifully landscaped grounds.

Ste. Genevieve Church, at Ste. Genevieve. Catholic. 1876. The present church marks the site of a church dating back to 1794, one of the first churches in the territory.

Trinity Lutheran Church, Altenburg. 1839; present church 1866. This is the mother-church of the Evangelical Lutheran Synod in the midwest.

St. Patrick's, St. Patrick. Catholic. 1954. This is the saint's shrine in the United States, and was constructed with contributions from every nation in the world.

St. John Nepomuc, St. Louis. Bohemian Catholic. 1854; present church 1896. The oldest Bohemian Catholic Church in the world outside of Czechoslovakia, this is looked upon as the mother-church of the many Slavic national churches in the United States.

St. Francis Xavier, Kansas City. Catholic. Recent. Designed by Barry Byrne and Parke, this modern structure is formed to resemble a fish, an ancient symbol for Christ.

Church of the Resurrection, St. Louis. 1950's. An unusual example of modern design.

MONTANA

St. Ignatius Mission, St. Ignatius. Catholic. First church 1854; present church 1891. Mission founded by the Jesuit de Smet to serve the Flathead Indians.

St. Paul's, Virginia City. Episcopal. 1867. The first Episcopal church in the state.

St. Mary's Mission, Stevensville. Catholic. 1841; present building 1866. Early mission; once served as parish church.

Cathedral of St. Helena, Helena. Catholic. 1914. Cathedral built in pure Gothic style, patterned after Cathedral of Cologne, Germany, and famed for its stained glass and Carrara marble.

St. Peter's, procathedral, Helena. Episcopal. 1931. Noted for its stained glass windows, which depict in part the history of the state.

St. Charles, Whitefish. Catholic. 1955. A new and ultra-modern church.

St. Gabriel's Church, Chinook. 1885; present church 1955. A prize-winning small church of modern design.

NEBRASKA

Methodist Church, Brownville. 1858. One of the first churches in the area to follow the "arbor churches."

First Presbyterian Church, Bellevue. 1856. An early church, largely rebuilt in 1904.

St. Cecelia's Cathedral, Omaha. Catholic. 1908. An outstanding example of Romanesque architecture, known for its statue of "Our Lady of Nebraska" and chapel.

Trinity Church, Omaha. Episcopal. 1856. Cathedral; the first Episcopal church in the state.

Cathedral of the Nativity of the Blessed Virgin Mary, Grand Island. Catholic. 1928. Noteworthy for its beautiful design.

NEVADA

Cathedral of St. Thomas Aquinas, Reno. Catholic. 1907. Designed and constructed in Baroque style, the mural paintings are considered to be among the nation's finest.

St. Mary's in the Mountains, Virginia City. Catholic. 1860; present church 1876. This church is known as the "Glory of the Comstock." It is famous for its high oak vaulting.

St. Paul's, Virginia City. Episcopal. 1861. The first Episcopal church in the state.

St. Augustine's, Austin. Catholic. 1868. Interesting tower and steeple. This church stands in a modern "ghost town" as a relic of the mining days.

NEW HAMPSHIRE

St. George's Episcopal Church, Durham. 1950's. Contemporary modern, designed by the architect John A. Carter.

St. John's Church, Portsmouth. Episcopal. 1732, present church 1807.
Classic brick colonial church.

NEW JERSEY

Old First Presbyterian Church, Newark. 1666; present structure 1791.
Famed early church in the state, it was served by Aaron Burr, Sr.,
as pastor from 1736 to 1755.

First Presbyterian Church, Springfield. 1745; present building 1791.
This church was on the scene of the Revolutionary War battle of
Springfield, June 23, 1780. The Reverend James Caldwell rallied the
patriots by tearing up the hymnals for gun wadding.

St. Mary's, Burlington. Episcopal. 1703. St. Mary's Hall for girls was
founded in 1837, perhaps the first institution of its kind in the country.

Quaker Meeting House, Crosswicks. 1773. Used both as barracks and
hospital by the Hessian soldiers after the Revolutionary War battle
of June 23, 1778, this church still has a cannonball embedded in the
north wall.

St. Peter's, Perth Amboy. Episcopal. 1685. The first Episcopal church in
the state.

Old Tennent Church, Freehold. Quaker. 1751. Became famous during
the battle of Monmouth. Here Molly Pitcher replaced her husband
at the cannon when he fell.

Sacred Heart Cathedral, Newark. Catholic. 1898. An outstanding example of French Gothic style.

St. John's, Newark. Catholic. 1827. Oldest Catholic church still in use
in the state.

NEW MEXICO

Cathedral of St. Francis of Assisi, Santa Fe. Catholic. 1610; present
building (supplanting two previous adobe churches) 1866. This was
built by Bishop Lamy, featured in Willa Cather's novel, *Death Comes
for the Archbishop.*

San Esteban ("Old Mission of Acoma"), Acoma Pueblo. Catholic. c. 1629.
This mission, built of adobe and immense log beams, is set atop a
standing rock four hundred feet above the desert.

St. Joseph, Old Laguna. Catholic. 1699. An early mission, this has a striking interior. Situated on the route of the Santa Fe Railroad, this mission is perhaps the best known of all.

Catholic Missions. No less than twenty-four were erected between 1580 and 1838. Many are now in ruins.

St. Paul's, Las Vegas. Episcopal. 1879. The first Episcopal church in the state.

Montefiore Synagogue, Las Vegas. 1884. An early Jewish center in the west, this is to be disbanded in the near future.

NEW YORK

John Street Methodist Church, Wall Street district, New York City. 1766; present building 1841. Oldest Methodist congregation and society in America.

Cathedral of St. John the Divine, New York City. Episcopal. 1892; still being built. This building will be the largest church in America and the largest Gothic cathedral in the world.

St. Patrick's Cathedral, New York City. Catholic. 1858–79. America's first major cathedral built in Gothic Revival style, this is the diocesan cathedral of the Cardinal Archbishop of the city.

Trinity Church, New York City. Episcopal. Founded in 1697 by Royal Charter; present building consecrated in 1846. The first Episcopal church in the city, its steeple has long served as a landmark of the Wall Street district.

St. Paul's Chapel of Trinity Parish, New York City. Episcopal. 1766. This is the oldest church building in Manhattan, built of stone quarried from what is now the cemetery. It was to this church that George Washington repaired after his inauguration on April 30, 1789, where Bishop Samuel Provoost conducted the service.

St. Luke's Chapel, New York City. Episcopal. Original church 1822; part of Trinity Church Parish since 1892. A recently-completed program has renovated and rebuilt the city block surrounding the chapel for parish use; a new school is among the community of buildings.

Marble Collegiate Church, New York City. Dutch Reformed. Founded 1628; present church 1854. Oldest Protestant church in North America with continuous ministry since its founding. Peter Minuit was its first elder; its present pastor, installed in 1932, is Dr. Norman Vincent Peale.

The Church of the Transfiguration, New York City. Protestant Episcopal. 1848. Known as the "Little Church Around the Corner," this church is a favorite among theatrical people.

St. Mark's-in-the-Bouwerie, New York City. Dutch. Founded in 1660; last remodeled in 1858. Built as the chapel on the farm of the Governor, Peter Stuyvesant, it has remained as an early mark of the city's history. The Stuyvesant family is buried here.

St. Peter's, New York City. Catholic. 1785. The first Catholic church in the city.

St. Joseph's, New York City. Catholic. 1833. Notable example of neo-classic art.

Sacred Heart, Hartsdale. Catholic. An excellent example of contemporary design.

St. Mary's, Albany. Catholic. 1797; present church 1867. The first parish church between New York and Buffalo.

St. Joseph's, Rochester. Catholic. 1846. Originally named St. Mary's, the parish was established in 1836 and was an eastern center for German-speaking Catholic immigrants.

St. Matthew's, New York City. Lutheran. 1648. The oldest Lutheran church in America.

First Baptist Church, Hamilton. 1825. A neo-classic church which is the mother-church of Colgate University.

The Riverside Church, New York City. 1925. An outstanding example of modern Gothic, notable for its beautiful windows.

New Dorp Moravian Church, Staten Island. 1844. Its famous cemetery contains the mausoleum of the Vanderbilt family.

Our Lady of Fatima, Scarsdale. Catholic. 1951. A church recognized for its modern design.

Bay Ridge Methodist Church, Ovington Avenue, Brooklyn. 1830. Built of rare green stone, this is the oldest Methodist church in Brooklyn.

K.T.I. Synagogue, Port Chester. 1950's. Modern design in good transition; Philip Johnson, architect.

Church of St. Andrew, Staten Island. Episcopal. Founded 1708; first building 1712, enlarged in 1743. Scene of Revolutionary War skirmishes. This church is part of noted Richmondtown restoration, now under way.

The Protestant Dutch Reformed Church of Flatlands, Brooklyn. 1654; present church 1848. Built on Kings Highway, this old colonial building stands where Revolutionary War armies passed on the fateful night of August 26, 1776. The church-bell dates from 1794.

Plymouth Church of the Pilgrims, Brooklyn. Congregational. 1844. Famous red-brick New England meeting-house style church, without tower or steeple. Henry Ward Beecher was its pastor from 1847 to 1887.

Temple Emanu-El, New York City. Synagogue (Reformed). Founded 1845; present temple 1929. Romanesque, with a two-domed chapel structure in Byzantine style.

Reformed Protestant Dutch Church of Flatbush, Brooklyn. 1655; present church 1796, renovated in 1926. Its bell gave warning of the approach of the British at the time of the battle of Long Island.

NORTH CAROLINA

Sandy Creek Baptist Church, Randolph County. Founded 1755; the church erected in 1800 still stands near the present structure. This is the mother-church of the Southern Baptists.

St. Thomas, Bath. Episcopal. 1734. The oldest church building in the state.

St. Paul's, Edenton. Episcopal. Parish founded in 1701; third building 1736. The site of the oldest Episcopal parish in the state.

Christ Church, Raleigh. Episcopal. 1848. Gothic Revival architecture.

Home Moravian Church, Old Salem. 1771; present building 1800. The center of Moravian activities of the Southern Province.

St. James', Wilmington. Episcopal. 1839. Designed by T. U. Walter, the architect of the national Capitol dome. This church contains a painting of the head of Christ, *Ecce Homo,* taken from a Spanish man-of-war that attacked the town of Brunswick in 1748. St. James' was also used as a hospital during the Union occupation of the town.

St. Paul's, New Bern. Catholic. A nineteenth-century church, perhaps the oldest Catholic church in the state.

Bethabara Moravian Church, rural Winston-Salem. Founded 1753; church built in 1788. The first Moravian church in the state.

NORTH DAKOTA

Christ Church, Fargo. Episcopal. 1877. Gethsemane Cathedral; the first Episcopal church in the state.

Cathedral of the Holy Spirit, Bismarck. Catholic. 1945. A poured-concrete structure, first of the kind in the Northwest.

St. Mary's, Medora. Catholic. 1884. Built by the Marquis de Mores, who was a friend of President Theodore Roosevelt.

Church of the Assumption of the Blessed Virgin Mary, Pembina. Catholic. First church, no longer extant, 1818.

OHIO

St. Luke's Church, Granville. Episcopal. 1819; present church 1837. Classic design in a type of Early American architecture.

Grace Evangelical Lutheran, Fremont. 1892; present church, 1899–1929. This Gothic cathedral is of classic design and is the primary church of the Sandusky valley.

Christ Protestant Episcopal Church, Hudson. 1802; present building 1930. An example of pure Georgian architecture, the present building contains much of the earlier church.

Grace Methodist Church, Dayton. Founded 1797; first structure 1812; present (fifth) structure 1921. This church, the result of early missionary work, is English Gothic with Flemish detail.

Breckville Congregational Church, Breckville. 1844. A pioneer church of its period.

Plum Street Temple, Cincinnati. Jewish. Organized 1824; present building 1866. Hailed as the first and finest synagogue of its kind in the country.

The Temple: Reorganized Church of Latter-day Saints, Kirtland. 1834. A fine example of late colonial architecture, this is one of the most striking church structures of the state.

First Congregational Church, Tallmadge. Founded 1809; built in 1822. Said to be the oldest church of continuous use as a place of worship in the state.

Mount Pleasant Meeting House, Mount Pleasant. Society of Friends. 1814. A historic building in the sense that Quakers fleeing the pro-slavery activity of the South came to this new country to find an atmosphere of freedom.

Moravian Mission Church, Schoenbrunn. 1722. Ohio's earliest church established for the Christian Indians, now reconstructed and administered by the Ohio Historical Society.

St. Peter in Chains Cathedral, Cincinnati. Catholic. 1821; present church 1845. The first cathedral of the first Ohio bishop, Edward Fenwick, this church of classic Greek style has just been rebuilt.

Church of St. Joseph, Somerset. Catholic. Log church 1818; present church 1840, repaired after fire of 1866. The first Catholic church in the state.

College First Church of God, Findlay. Churches of God in North America. 1949. Third offshoot of the group founded in Harrisburg, Pennsylvania, by Elder John Winebrenner in 1830.

Christ Church, Cincinnati. Christian. 1950's. Fine modern architecture; Saarinen, Saarinen and Associates, architects.

St. John's, Worthington. Episcopal. 1804. The first Episcopal church in the state.

OKLAHOMA

St. Patrick's, Lockridge. Catholic. Early 1800's. Perhaps the oldest extant Catholic church in the state.

First Christian Church, Oklahoma City. Christian. 1955. A departure from the traditional, this church is startlingly designed. R. Duane Conner, architect.

Trinity Church, Guthrie. Episcopal. 1889. The first Episcopal church in the state.

Boston Avenue Methodist Church, Tulsa. Founded 1900; present (third) church, 1929. Designed by the Quaker artist, Miss Adah Robinson, this church is modern and of vast proportions.

OREGON

West Union Baptist Church, West Union. 1853. Claimed to be the first Baptist church west of the Rocky Mountains.

Rock Creek Methodist Church, Molalla. 1852. Dedicated as a historic shrine in 1939.

Trinity Church, Portland. Episcopal. 1851; present church 1872. The
first Episcopal parish in the Pacific northwest.

Central Lutheran Church, Portland. 1950's. Contemporary design by
Pietro Belluschi.

PENNSYLVANIA

NOTE: The state of Pennsylvania embraces more than one hundred
churches, all of which are listed by county in the *Catalog of Historical
Buildings, Sites and Remains in Pennsylvania* prepared by the Joint
State Government Commission to the General Assembly, 1949. The fol-
lowing churches comprise only a partial list of those presented in the
Catalog, but included are those considered of notable significance.

St. Paul Monastery Church, Pittsburgh. Catholic. Early 1800's. The first
Passionist Fathers foundation in the United States.

First Church of God, Harrisburg. Churches of God in North America.
1854. The mother-church of this denomination in the United States.

St. Michael's, Loretto. Catholic. Founded 1799; present 1899. This
church was founded by the famous prince-priest, Demetrius Augustine
Gallitzin.

Cathedral of St. Peter and St. Paul, Philadelphia. Catholic. 1846. The
cathedral is famed for its architecture.

Old St. Mary's, Philadelphia. Catholic. 1763. Historic church where
John Barry is buried.

Old St. Joseph, Philadelphia. Catholic. 1733. The first Catholic church
in the city, this was built on land purchased in 1722.

St. Michael, Philadelphia. Catholic. 1833. Figured in the Nativist riot
in May, 1844.

St. Augustine, Philadelphia. Catholic. 1796. An old church which suffered in the Nativist riot of May, 1844.

St. Philip Neri, Philadelphia. Catholic. 1840. Figured in the Nativist
riot of 1844.

Holy Trinity, Philadelphia. Catholic. 1789. The first German national
church in the United States.

St. Mary Magdalen de Pazzi, Philadelphia. Catholic. 1852. The first
Italian national church in the United States.

St. Anne, Philadelphia. Catholic. 1845. Noted for its stained glass windows and Stations of the Cross, which are works of art.

East Liberty Presbyterian Church, Pittsburgh. 1819; present building 1935. A classic Gothic church with lavish appointments.

Christ Church, Philadelphia. Episcopal. Founded 1695; present church 1754. Benjamin Franklin was a pew holder here. He and six other signers of the Declaration of Independence are buried in the church-yard. Declared a national shrine in 1950.

The Great Conewago Presbyterian Church, near McSherrystown. 1787. One of the oldest Presbyterian churches still in use.

Exeter Friends Meetinghouse, near Stonersville. 1759. An old stone meeting house in whose churchyard are buried the ancestors of Abraham Lincoln and Daniel Boone.

Harmony Mennonite Church, near Zelienople. 1825. A church built by successors of the Harmony Society.

First Presbyterian Church, Carlisle. Founded 1734; erected c. 1755. A stone church, and historical landmark.

Donegal Church, near Elizabethtown. Presbyterian. Founded 1714; built c. 1740. Site of the Witness Tree, where the congregation made an avowal of patriotism in 1777.

Bryn Athyn Cathedral, Bryn Athyn. Swedenborgian. 1914. Center of the faith, this is noted for its Gothic and Romanesque architecture.

Merion Meetinghouse, Ardmore. Quaker. 1695. One of the two existing churches where William Penn preached; still in use.

Gemein Haus, Bethlehem. Lutheran. 1741. Marked by the Pennsylvania Historical and Museum Commission, 1931.

First Church of the Brethren, Germantown. Dunker. 1770. Mother-church of the Dunker sect in America. Bibles printed by Christopher Sauer which were stored in the church were used as gun wadding by British soldiers at the battle of Germantown.

Old St. George's Methodist Church, Philadelphia. 1763; present build-ing 1769. Begun by Dutch Presbyterian church; completed by the Methodist Society. Scene of first Methodist Society Conference, July 14, 1773.

"The Old Chapel," Bethlehem. Moravian. 1751. The first building used as a place of worship by the Moravians in America. In it, Benjamin Franklin, George Washington, and other colonial leaders worshiped.

Central Moravian Church, Bethlehem. 1803. The "home congregation" of the Northern Province of the Moravian Church worships here. Out-standing example of colonial architecture.

Old Norriton Presbyterian Church, Norristown. 1678; present church

1698. One of the oldest Presbyterian churches extant in the United States.

St. John's Church, Allentown. Lutheran. 1855. Modern Gothic. Congregation known for its multi-racial educational ministries.

Augustus Church, Collegeville. Lutheran. 1743. Known as "The Trappe," this church was erected by the patriarch of American Lutheranism, the Rev. Dr. Henry Melchior Muhlenberg.

RHODE ISLAND

Touro Synagogue, Newport. Dedicated 1763. The oldest synagogue in the United States; designed by Peter Harrison. Dedicated as a national historical site in 1947.

First Baptist Church, Newport. 1774. Called the mother-church of the Baptist denomination in this country. Designed by Joseph Brown.

Trinity Church, Newport. Episcopal. 1726. Designed by Peter Harrison, this church won fame during the American Revolution.

St. Paul's, Wickford. Episcopal. 1707. The oldest Episcopal church in the northern United States; no longer in use.

Sabbatarian Meeting House, Newport. Baptist. 1729. Oldest Seventh-Day Baptist church in the country.

Quaker Meeting House, Newport. Late 1600's. The oldest church building in the state, this is the state's sole remaining example of hip-roofed and turreted meeting houses built at the time.

Elder Ballou Meeting House, Cumberland. Six-principle Baptist. 1749. This remains in an excellent state of preservation, practically unchanged.

Old Colony House, Newport. Where the General Assembly met in Newport; served briefly as a church when the first Catholic Mass was read there in 1780, when a French chaplain consecrated the building.

St. Mary's, Newport. Catholic. 1852. Notable for its Gothic style.

The First Baptist Church in America, Providence. Founded in 1638 by Roger Williams; present church dedicated in 1775. Oldest church in the state, and the oldest Baptist church in America.

First Hopkinton Seventh-Day Baptist Church, Ashaway. 1680; present church 1835. Sabbatarian church, chartered by the state in 1708. Mother-church of the denomination.

SOUTH CAROLINA

First Baptist Church, Charleston. Early 1800's. The first Baptist church organized south of Philadelphia; notable architecturally.

St. Philip's, Charleston. Episcopal. 1670. The first Episcopal church in the state.

Circular Church, Charleston. Congregational. 1681. Oldest Congregational church in the state.

SOUTH DAKOTA

Bon Homme Congregational Church, near Tabor. 1870. This stands on the site of the old town, now deserted, although the church is still used. Back of the church is a replica of the first school in the state.

Richland Church, Richland. Christian. 1866. Claimed to be the first church structure in South Dakota.

Christ Church, Yankton. Episcopal. 1862. The first Episcopal church in the state.

Presbyterian Indian Church, Flandreau. 1873. Built by a group of Christian Santee Indians after they left the Reservation to homestead in the area.

Sacred Heart Church, Parkston. Catholic. Late 1800's. One of the first permanent church structures in the state.

TENNESSEE

First Baptist Church, Clinton. 1840; present church 1883. Church which figured in a controversy over doctrine between Baptists and Methodists.

St. Peter's, Memphis. Catholic. Founded 1839; dedicated 1858. The first Catholic church in the city.

First Methodist Church, Memphis. 1826; present church 1880. Held to be the "finest sanctuary in the state."

St. Paul's, Franklin. Episcopal. 1827. The first Episcopal church in the state.

St. Mary's, Nashville. Catholic. 1844. The first cathedral of the state and the oldest Catholic church in Nashville.

TEXAS

San Fernando Cathedral, San Antonio. Catholic. 1738. The oldest parish church in Texas.

St. David's, Austin. Episcopal. 1854. The oldest Protestant church in Austin.

Mission of the Immaculate Conception, San Antonio. Catholic. 1730. Claimed to be the first church in the United States dedicated to the Immaculate Conception of the Blessed Mother.

Mission San Jose y San Miguel de Aguayo, near San Antonio. Catholic. 1720; present church 1768. Considered one of the finest examples of mission architecture erected in New Spain.

Mission San Antonio de Valero (The Alamo), San Antonio. Originally a Catholic mission, founded in 1718. Hailed as the "Cradle of Texas."

Mission San Francisco de la Espada, San Antonio. Catholic. 1730. Early Spanish mission.

Other Catholic missions:

San Juan Capistrano, San Antonio. 1730.

La Bahia del Espiritu Santo, Goliad. 1749.

Corpus Christi de la Isleta del Sur (Nuestra Señora del Monte Carmelo), Ysleta. 1682.

Nuestra Señora del Socorro, Socorro. 1683.

Presidio de San Elizario, San Elizario. 1773.

Christ Church, Matagorda. Episcopal. 1839. The first Episcopal church in the state.

First Baptist Church, Dallas. 1915. The largest Baptist membership and greatest mission contribution in the world.

Trinity Episcopal Church, Galveston. 1841; present building 1855. Pioneer church of eastern Texas.

Church of Christ the King, Dallas. Catholic. 1955. Excellent adapted contemporary design.

UTAH

Temple of Salt Lake City. Church of Jesus Christ of Latter-day Saints (Mormon). Begun 1853; completed 1893. This many-spired temple is the "home" temple of Mormonism.

The Box Elder Stake Tabernacle, Brigham City. Mormon. 1876.

Other Mormon temples:
  Manti Temple, Manti. 1879.
  Logan Temple, Logan. 1877–84.
  St. George Temple, St. George. 1871–77.
  Tabernacle, Salt Lake City. 1863–67.
  Summit Stake Tabernacle, Coalville. 1877.
  Cedar City Chapel, Cedar City. 1931–34.
St. Mark's, Salt Lake City. Episcopal. 1867. The first Episcopal church
  in the state.
Cathedral of the Madeleine, Salt Lake City. Catholic. 1900. The Catholic
  diocesan center.

VERMONT

Old Meeting House (First Church in Rockingham), near Bellows Falls.
  1787. The oldest church of continuous service in Vermont.
Old First Church of Bennington, Old Bennington. Congregational. 1805.
  Called "Vermont's Colonial Shrine," this is one of the most beautiful
  colonial churches in New England.
St. James', Arlington. Episcopal. 1772. The first Episcopal church in the
  state.
Old Round Church, Richmond. 1813. This sixteen-sided building was
  the first community church in the territory. Now used as a town office.
Blessed Sacrament, Stowe. Catholic. 1949. A small modern church dedicated to Brother Ira Dutton for his work among the lepers of Molokai;
  noted for its art.

VIRGINIA

St. Peter's, near Richmond. Episcopal. 1703. Known as the "First church
  of the first First Lady." George Washington was married here.
Jamestown Church, Jamestown Island. Episcopal. 1607. Dissolved in
  1812. At present this church (the third, built in 1699) is a shrine.
Bruton Parish Church, Williamsburg. Episcopal. 1674; present church,
  a restoration, built in 1711.
St. Luke's, Smithfield. 1630. The oldest Protestant church on United
  States soil.

Pohick Church, Fairfax County. Episcopal. 1730; rebuilt in 1768. George Washington was a parishioner here.

Sacred Heart Cathedral, Richmond. Catholic. 1903. Fine example of Italian Renaissance architecture.

St. Mary's, Alexandria. Catholic. 1795; present church 1860; repaired after fire in 1891. The first permanent Catholic church in the state.

St. William of York Church, Aquia. Catholic. 1956. A commemorative church erected on the site of the first permanent Catholic settlement in Virginia, 1647.

St. Peter's, Richmond. Catholic. 1834. The Cathedral church of Cardinal Gibbons, and associated with the poet John Bannister Tabb.

First Baptist Church, Richmond. Present church 1925. Of architectural and historical importance.

WASHINGTON

St. Luke's, Vancouver. Episcopal. 1873. The first Episcopal church in the state.

Church of Grandview. Catholic. A fine example of today's architecture; designed by T. F. Hargis, Jr.

St. Elizabeth's, Burien. Episcopal. 1956. A prize-winning modern design; Durham, Anderson and Freed, architects.

WEST VIRGINIA

Old Stone Church, Lewisburg. Presbyterian. Founded in 1783; present stone building erected in 1796. The first church west of the Allegheny Mountains.

Rehoboth Church, Monroe County. Methodist. 1784. Dedicated in 1786 by the Reverend Francis Asbury.

Christ Church, Bunker Hill. Presbyterian. Erected in 1740 on the Morgan estate; present building 1853. The church of the first recorded settlement in the state.

WISCONSIN

First Unitarian Society Church, Madison. 1951. Unusual modern design by Frank Lloyd Wright.

St. Gabriel's Parish, Prairie du Chien. Catholic. c. 1817. The earliest organized parish in the state.

St. Joseph's, Madeline Island. Catholic. Founded 1665; present church 1864. The first church in Wisconsin; present church built by Bishop Baraga.

Christ Church, Green Bay. Episcopal. 1826. The first Episcopal church in the state.

St. Norbert, Roxbury. Catholic. 1857. A historic church which boasts an unusual painting.

St. Patrick's, Benton. Catholic. 1847. One of the churches built by Father Samuel C. Mazzuchelli; he is buried in its cemetery.

St. Augustine, New Diggings. Catholic. 1844. An early Mazzuchelli church.

St. Peter's, Milwaukee. Catholic. 1839. The first cathedral in the Northwest, this wooden frame building was dismantled and re-erected on the grounds of St. Francis Seminary in 1939.

Trinity Evangelical Lutheran Church, Thiensville. Founded 1839; present church 1884. The oldest Lutheran parish in Wisconsin.

St. Mary's, La Crosse. Catholic. 1855. An early Mississippi mission.

St. Paul's, Milwaukee. Episcopal. 1838; present church 1884. The pioneer Episcopal church in Wisconsin; its stained glass by Tiffany is widely admired.

St. Paul's Cathedral, Fond du Lac. Episcopal. Present structure 1885. Good English Gothic style.

Green Bay East Moravian Church, Green Bay. 1851. One of the first Moravian churches in the Midwest.

WYOMING

Church of the Transfiguration, Moose. Christian. 1914. This church looks out onto a magnificent view of the Grand Teton range.

St. Mary's Cathedral, Cheyenne. Catholic. 1908. A classic example of English Gothic style.

St. Mark's, Cheyenne. Episcopal. 1868. The first Episcopal church in the state.

Index

HISTORIC CHURCHES OF THE UNITED STATES

HISTORIC
CHURCHES
OF THE UNITED STATES

by Robert C. Broderick

DRAWINGS BY VIRGINIA BRODERICK

CARL A. RUDISILL LIBRARY
LENOIR RHYNE COLLEGE

WILFRED FUNK, INC., NEW YORK

© *1958 by Wilfred Funk, Inc.*
Library of Congress Catalog Card Number 58–7142
Printed in the United States of America
Designed by Betty Crumley

726.5
B 78h

40191
October, 1960

My foot hath stood in the direct way:
in the churches I will bless Thee, O Lord.

—PS. 25:12

Contents

Illustrations

ACKNOWLEDGMENTS

In writing a book of this kind, it is necessary to call upon the resources, patience, and kindness of many individuals. Much of this record of historic churches was available only from local sources, and, apart from visiting each place, I could not have done better than rely on those whose knowledge of each church was first-hand. I had also to call for aid from a number of historical societies and other sources. It is my desire to express my heartfelt gratitude to each and all, not in degree according to their assistance, but with unmeasured warmth.

First, my thanks to my wife, Virginia, for her fine contribution of art for the book, for her counsel, and for her silence in suffering the piles of material that gathered in our home.

My deep appreciation to Herman Ziegler; Peter Murphy; Dr. Clifford L. Lord, Wisconsin State Historical Society; Rev. Raphael Hamilton, S.J., Marquette University; Right Rev. Peter Leo Johnson, historian and author; Rev. P. J. Rahill,

St. Louis University; Rev. T. T. McAvoy, Notre Dame University; A. C. Outler, Southern Methodist University; Rev. P. H. Ahern, St. Paul Seminary; Rev. F. J. Kennedy, editor; and Boyd C. Shafer of the American Historical Association; all of whom were consulted early in the undertaking.

To E. J. Schulte, architect; Mrs. H. M. Ottman and *Architectural Forum;* Jeanne Davern and *Architectural Record;* E. L. Spencer and *Catholic Property Administration;* and Margaret Squire and *Progressive Architecture.*

To August R. Suelflow, Concordia Historical Institute; Right Rev. Kenneth G. Hamilton, Moravian Church in America; Henry Davis, Jr., Director of Religious Education; W. B. Davis, publication, Church of Christ, Scientist; Col. L. L. Cobb; W. B. Miller, Presbyterian Historical Society; E. C. Stone, American Baptist Historical Society; David Evans & Associates and M. E. Petersen, Church of Jesus Christ of Latter-day Saints; F. Eppling Reinartz, Secretary, United Lutheran Church in America; Mrs. D. J. White; H. P. Kellett; Rev. DuBose Murphy; Norman W. Cox, Baptist Historical Commission; K. E. Boldosser, Secretary, Churches of God in America; R. Gordon Spaugh, Moravian Church in America; W. H. Porter, American Baptist Convention; Eva Lois St. John, Seventh-day Baptist Historical Society; F. L. Fagley, Congregational Church Historical Society; E. B. Sloan, Arizona Pioneers' Historical Society; Lila Brady, Indiana State Library; C. C. Walton, Illinois State Historical Library; George S. May, Michigan Historical Commission; Charlotte Capers, Mississippi Department of Archives; D. H. Welsh, Missouri Historical Review; B. H. Wall, Southern Historical Association; Mrs. J. W. Brown; Cleofas Calleros; D. H. Kent, Pennsylvania Historical & Museum Commission; Mrs. Dale Thomas, West Virginia Department of History; Miss M. Gleason, Librarian, Wisconsin Historical Society; Rita Ridings, Wyoming History Department; Mrs. G. M. Wood.

And to the following members of State Historical Societies: James de T. Abajian, California; J. D. Morrison, Colorado; Ruthanna Hindes, Delaware; H. J. Swinney, Idaho; William J. Peterson, Iowa; Alberta Pantle, Kansas; G. G. Clift, Kentucky; Marian B. Rowe, Maine; Stewart Mitchell, Massachusetts; Charles van Ravenswaay, Missouri; Virginia Walton, Montana; A. G. Ely, New Mexico; H. W. Wiseman, New Jersey; J. J. Heslin, New York; James H. Rodabough, Ohio; W. D. Aeschbacher, Nebraska; Miss C. D. Canover, New Hampshire; Rucker Agee, Alabama; E. C. Zepp, Ohio; Priscilla Knuth, Oregon; C. P. Monahon, Rhode Island; W. G. Robinson, South Dakota; H. B. Carroll, Texas; A. R. Mortensen, Utah; R. G. Wood, Vermont.

Special thanks to the members of the Chancery offices who replied to my requests for information and photographs; and to the directors of church groups and their staffs. In particular, my thanks to C. A. Anderson, Presbyterian Church Department of History; William J. Moll, Episcopal Director of Public Relations; Dean Wilson, Helena, Montana; Rev. A. O. Kaltwasser; Rev. G. L. Utterback; Rev. James H. Viggers; Horace Holley, Secretary, National Spiritual Assembly; Dr. Mohamed Bisar, Director of the Islamic Center; Mrs. M. L. Main, Director of Publicity for Washington Cathedral; Edward C. Starr, American Baptist Historical Society; Rev. H. L. Trickett; Rabbi Theodore Lewis; Helen Rose Cline; Rev. R. C. Hunsicker; Rev. Bruce W. Evans; Rev. R. A. Pfrangle; Rev. Edward A. De Miller; Rev. A. J. Lewis; Rev. E. H. Gibson; Margaret A. Guthrie; H. Whitfield; Rev. C. H. Douglass; Rev. Randolph Ray; Rabbi R. B. Gittelsohn; B. I. Pincus; Edna M. Osborn; Rhodes Thompson; Mrs. Helen W. Stearns; William O. Hackett; Rev. P. A. Kellog; Raul Lyon; Violet T. Motley; Rev. Arne Christianson; Rev. M. D. Gaebler; Rev. T. K. Smith; Rev. F. M. Meek; Dr. Ralph Stoody, E. P. Watson.

And to Most Rev. J. F. Flannelly; Rev. R. T. Carpenter, C.S.P.; Rev. J. A. Haugh; Rev. M. M. Hoffman; Very Rev. Charles W. Popell; Rev. R. J. Monroe; Rev. E. M. Hanley, O.P.; Rev. E. A. Shanahan; Very Rev. G. E. Ryan; Rev. C. J. Graham; Rev. J. V. Casey; Rev. J. D. McClumn; Right Rev. J. J. Fitzpatrick; Rev. Michael Pascual, C.R.; Rev. L. McFadden; Right Rev. M. D. O'Connell; Rev. Celestine, O.F.M.; Right Rev. J. R. O'Donoghue; Rev. C. M. Williams; Rev. J. N. Gross; Rev. James Rizer; Rev. J. W. Love; Rev. T. F. Durkin; Rev. A. J. Vincent; Rev. Milton Schellenburg; Very Rev. W. F. Maloney, S.J.; Rev. J. Gallagher; Rev. J. A. Duskie; Rev. A. C. Smith, S.J.; Rev. Robert Gorman; Rev. N. J. Curran; Sister M. Claudia, O.S.B.; Rev. J. G. Hogan, S.J.; Rev. J. P. Hough.

And finally, but with no lesser degree of gratitude, my appreciation to the editors, designers of the book, and to the photographers and printers; and to all those who have aided in any measure, but who through my fallibility have not received a more direct word from me. To all, a prayerful thanks.

PREFACE

In presenting this review of past and present churches, we have tried to sidestep the realm of sentimentality. If a tinge of sentiment does appear from time to time, however, it is only the reflection of what we feel to be a justifiable pride in the churches of our land. Our churches have served us well, continue to serve. More than any other buildings which may reach architecturally skyward, our churches express our most worthy aspirations. They represent concretely our national wealth of spiritual principles, a wealth based, paradoxically, on the selfless giving of man's goods to foster the ideal of a nation under God. Without the aid, or the trammels, of state financing, our churches express the free response of free men.

We are concerned here with historic churches, but as we use this term, it has a rather wide area of reference. This book might properly be called a history of churches in the

United States. We could not, therefore, be satisfied merely with the chronological approach: the oldest church, the longest preserved. Instead, we look upon all churches as more or less "historic." If we were to write of the "history of musical instruments," we would encompass all from the first tympanum to the cymbal and lyre, and to the electrified instruments of today. So with our review of churches, our intention is to survey, from the earliest missions to the latest cathedrals, the place of churches in our history; we even dare some conjecture of the future. In considering the present, we must keep in mind that what expresses modernity in any age is really a modification of an older concept, that our religious esthetics have a basis in tradition.

By the word "church," as used herein, we mean a building rather than the following it represents. The word church used to mean "a congregation of people who meet periodically for religious services," thus referring to the believers who practiced the faith. This distinction was made in order to avoid confusion between the random crowds who came together occasionally to hear itinerant preachers or missionaries, and those regular groups of the faithful who only lacked a church building. A second meaning applied to "church" is: the aggregate of many "congregations"—making the word more or less a synonym for "denomination" or "sect" or "faith." Today, when organization serves to bring many groups to accept a particular discipline or teaching, the latter meaning is more widely used.

But our concern in this book is with the *house* of worship, and its place and time of construction. Thus we shall not discourse on the teachings of the various denominations or faiths. Our interest is in the historic, the artistic, the architectural, rather than in a doctrinal approach to our survey. In passing we may refer to missionary or other activity, but only to indicate its historic aspect.

Aware of the broadness of our task, we lay no claim to being all-inclusive: many churches have undoubtedly been overlooked here, and necessarily so. According to the 1958 edition of the *Yearbook of American Churches,* there are some 258 separate religious bodies in the continental United States with a total claimed membership of 100,162,529 persons. From the same source we learn that these millions worship in local churches numbering 308,647. It is obvious that, faced with such figures, we would find it impossible to be exhaustive in our presentation.

We plead, however, that our selection of churches featured here is not arbitrary; we were guided by the considered recommendations of historians, church or denomination authorities, architects and architectural journals, and church leaders. The final selection was based on our wish to present in feasible form the most representative, most interesting picture gleanable from an almost limitless panorama. One problem you will appreciate arose from the fact that a church building sometimes changed hands, passing from one denomination to another. Thus a church erected by a Presbyterian group may now serve a Congregational or other body. Then, too, in the space of decades, havoc has been wrought by fire and other disasters. Even in the course of this book's writing, some buildings which were originally listed have been destroyed. We have tried to portray only those churches which continue in use, but again, in spite of our care, one or another may already have passed from the scene.

We realize also that more churches will soon have been built, supplanting and surpassing our present selection of modern edifices. Our total number of churches is increasing by about one percent each year at an annual expenditure of some four billions of dollars. Along with this growth in facilities, church membership is increasing at a great pace; so great, in fact, that were all members to attend their churches, synagogues, and chapels regularly, present accommodations would be far from adequate.

Through this book, we seek to instill in each reader an appreciation of what churches have meant to this country in its historic expansion. At the same time we hope to demonstrate their contribution to our artistic and architectural heritage. May this book, then, serve as an introduction to many churches which you may never have seen, and as your invitation to visit them in the course of your travels. We offer this book for ourselves and for you, dedicating it to the Master of all builders and all artists, and to all who humbly pay Him homage.

The author

INTRODUCTION

It was not to a religiously barren land that our forebears came. Anthropologically there is no place on earth where one could find no form of worship of a deity. The innate need of man to worship, be it the sun, the moon, the forces of nature, or the true God revealed to man, has a universality like no other practice of the tribes of man. And America, the land of promise to many, the Mercatorian Indies, the New World, was not an exception. We have the remnants of some of the ancient "churches" of the natives; they survive today, as Indian memorials, in the flat-roofed Kivas of the Southwest Indian tribes. While these are recognized to be Indian religious temples, the practices of worship remain unknown. Kivas of the Southwest can be found in the vicinity of Bland, New Mexico, where a "ceremonial cave" was certainly a place of religious rites. Others are the "Large Kiva" in the Bandelier National Monument, and the Kivas in the Nambe and San Ildefonso pueblos of New Mexico.

Like other new lands, America was from the beginning looked upon as a "mission" land. The Spanish, eager and zealous Catholics, established the first two missions on what is now continental United States, at Timucua, Florida, in 1567, and at Guale in 1569—the latter in what is now the State of Georgia. From 1567 to 1861, more than ten religious denominations had erected missions for the Indians from Maine to the Pacific. These missions were frequently the forerunners of habitation and expansion by white settlers. The era of missions to the natives closes with the first year of the Civil War, but some remain active today, still cultivating faith among the American Indians.

It should be pointed out that there was some overlapping of missionary purposes during the first sixty years of the nineteenth century, when missions to the natives became, in some cases, subordinate to the missions set up among the many immigrants who were now threading their way across the country.

It is most evident from early records that, while many men had come to this new land in search of religious freedom, cooperation between church and government was essential. Only this cooperative effort, considering the common need for protection and sustenance, could have led to the successful settlement of the new continent. But the religious history of the United States as a nation is unique in many respects. Our early churches grew in an atmosphere of austerity and rebellion; yet their influence did much to transform the wilderness and weld diverse peoples into a nation. In fact, it is scarcely conceivable that any force, ideological or political, could have succeeded in unifying the new country had it not been supported by an underlying spiritual concept.

Among the earliest exploring groups and communities of settlers, ministers of religion were numbered; the strength of their determination to plant seeds of faith in the New World is apparent in the fact that early charters and land grants were drawn up with the provision that conversion of the natives and a direct fostering of the church be conditions of the papers of grant. It followed naturally that spiritual and religious ideals were to be incorporated into our Declaration of Independence, Constitution, and Bill of Rights. Studies have not yet been made, except locally, to estimate the great contribution made by religion, the presence of churches, to the fiber and structure of this nation.

At the places of earliest permanent settlement on this continent, we find churches. These "roofs for prayer" often had to serve a utilitarian purpose as strongholds against marauders, or as places of community sanctuary in time of disaster. No trace remains of many of these earliest churches, and their records are obscure. The earliest buildings erected for the religious use of English churchmen, so far as existent records show, were those on Roanoke Island in the territory of Virginia and at Sagadahoc at the mouth of the Kennebec River, in what is now the State of Maine. Neither of these buildings has survived, having been constructed of logs and intended to be supplanted by more permanent structures.

The first permanent settlement of colonists was at Jamestown in Virginia, which in 1957 celebrated the three hundred and fiftieth year of its founding. The location was some fifty miles above the mouth of the James River, the year 1607. The first rector was the Reverend Robert Hunt, an Anglican priest who had been rector of Reculver in the county of Kent, England. An old document describes the first church, which undoubtedly was supplanted by another. The chronicler writes: "When I first went to Virginia, I well remember we did hang an awning, an old sail, to three or four trees to shadow us from the sun; our walls were rails of wood, our seats unhewed planks until we cut planks, our pulpit a bar of wood nailed to two neighboring trees. This was our church till we built a homely thing like a barn, set upon crotchets, covered with rafts, sedges and earth, so were also the walls. Yet we had daily Common Prayer morning and evening, every Sunday two sermons, and every three months the Holy Communion, till our Minister died. But our Prayers daily, with an Homily on Sundays, we continued two or three years after till more Preachers came."

This brief account reveals how essential to the settlers were religion and a church. The "barn" passed on, but these words bring to life for us the spirit of the vigorous faith that built it. The Spring *News Letter* of The Congregational Historical Society sums up the significance of this beginning; in an article on Jamestown, Mr. Frederick L. Fagley writes: ". . . the American heritage includes the first representative legislature constituted in America which met in the Church at Jamestown, June 30, 1619, where it proceeded to 'draft laws for the government of the community.' Let us also remember that the Bill of Rights, drafted by Colonel George Mason of Virginia, became a model for other state constitutions and finally for the Constitution of the United States. During the first two hundred years, from Jamestown in 1607 to Madison's administration, the leaders of Virginia and New England lived and worked in close harmony. . . . Through all these years of the formation of American social and political idealism these two movements—little Jamestown in Virginia and little Plymouth and Boston Bay in New England—carried together the torch of freedom and fashioned the foundations of American idealism."

In a very real manner the early churches served to foster the ideals of the new settlers and work them into the developing substance of the American republic. The church building itself often served literally, as an early name implies, as a "meeting house" for the settlers—not only a place of worship, but a discussion center, a social hub. Churches became assembly points for those eager to learn the ways of self-government, and to speak freely their personal convictions.

We must not fail to recognize the early and continuing service that churches have given to our nation, nor to pay tribute to the men who have devoted themselves to church leadership. Now, as in the past, the preachers, ministers, rabbis, priests, and bishops as professional people of religion are a class apart. Outstanding in their culture and learning, they have been and continue to be deeply concerned with the cultivation of the ideals we all cherish. This is why much of the history of churches must be centered about these persons; it has so often been they who have made their churches memorable.

The numerous churches and chapels which span our country are varied in their expression of our national culture. In style some of these churches reflect nationality characteristics. In architecture they may demonstrate the influence of the topography, climate, and available building materials of their surroundings. While much church design and structure is derivative, can be traced to European or Eastern antecedents, it is becoming dramatically evident that we are beginning to advance toward a truly "American" type of church building.

The development of a national culture is reflected in our churches. They are not only an expression of the artistic conceptions of any given point in our history; sociologically, some historians maintain, churches provide a key to the quality of life and thought in any community. This is to say that, within the limits imposed by practicalities, we put into our churches our best craftsmanship and art—art intended to express what we feel to be the atmosphere of worship. While we know the buildings are subordinate to their purpose, that of providing a center for community worship, we have been striving to make them more beautiful. In this pursuit we can learn much from the past, if we will, and plan better for the future.

It is true that in building churches Americans have been somewhat sentimental, particularly about holding to traditional forms. We have been original, but only in degree, and esteem for the past becomes sterile when imitation alone remains. We could not hope to achieve a living art in our churches were we to feel so in awe of the past that we dared not attempt our own interpretation of the "atmosphere of prayer."

Let us build our kind of church, never fearing a new expression of art only because it is new. Because great art is a function of life, such art must be used to record our own historic present. We must use our creative talent, not only in our secular lives, but—as our forebears used it—in the service of our faith. While we recognize the beauty of past accomplishments, we must strive for our own through the employment of new techniques, skills, and materials which will truly express our religious aspirations.

An early midwestern abbot, the Benedictine Boniface Wimmer, in declaring for the necessity of the fine arts in our schools, states the case quite roundly: "Art must go hand in hand with religion, to give the exercises of religion that external splendor, dignity, and sublimity which make them more meaningful to sensuous man who cannot enter deeply enough into their inner spirit and therefore does not feel attracted to them."

The richness of our gifts in materials and means will not make up for a poverty of artistic intelligence. We must cultivate our national genius. But lest we fall into the error of being satisfied with mere novelty of shape or design, let us remember that our architecture will represent us to future historians; let us make it truly representative.

Many of our churches are the work of such great architects of the past as Bulfinch and Cram. We now look to the moderns: to Belluschi, Schulte, Byrne, Frank Lloyd Wright, that master of the functional, and many others. Later in this book we will see some examples of the modern trend; these will help to illuminate our hopes for the church of the future. This objective was stated in *L'Art d' église* in 1956 as follows: "No architecture was made in one day. There is, as Scripture puts it, a time for every thing; there is a time for blooming and a time for sowing. The chance of our time lies but on the modest but conscious efforts of a basic restarting. The only chance which religious architecture of the XXth century has of finding itself lies first in its ability to apply itself to the search of order."

In reviewing the history of our churches and the role they have played in our national history, we find a better "record of the activity of men" than can be found solely in the records of battles and the lives of statesmen.

HISTORIC CHURCHES OF THE UNITED STATES

I

CHURCHES IN
EARLY AMERICAN HISTORY

We could not do better than begin this chapter with the earliest religious foundation on our continental United States. Located in north central Florida, to the north of the city of St. Augustine, this is the mission of Nombre de Dios (meaning "Name of God"). It was founded in 1565 by Father Francisco López de Mendoza Grajales, a chaplain assigned to the Spanish fleet commanded by Captain General Pedro Menéndez de Avilés. With the firmness of grip of a dedicated person, this mission has survived to the present day.

It was here in the Florida lowlands that the first Catholic Mass was offered for those who came to found our nation's first permanent settlement. The Spaniards were pious, but they were also bold and realistic. They were aware of the dangers from the natives and were soon to become aware of the precarious nature of possession when a new continent is opened to eager nations and treasure-seeking men.

At the Mission in the early seventeenth century, there was erected the Shrine of Nuestra Señora de la Leche y Buen Parto (Our Nursing Mother of Happy Delivery). Today this is the Catholic national Shrine of Christian Motherhood, and the symbol of its devotion is the little statue of the Blessed Mother nursing the Infant Christ, called the La Leche Statue.

The work of the Mission was, despite the natural hardships, successful. The Timucuan Indians accepted Christianity and became the exemplars of other tribes who failed to follow immediately the peace-loving "mission Indians." Natives from the north came down to battle the Spaniards grouped about the Mission, and in attacking in the vicinity of the settlement of St. Augustine, they bludgeoned to death Father Blas Rodriguez in 1597—after granting his plea to be allowed to finish the Sacrifice of the Mass.

More than a hundred years later, in 1728, while momentous stirrings were taking place to the north, an officer of King George, Colonel John Palmer, waded through the Georgian swamps, pillaged and burned the outer town of St. Augustine, and desecrated the Mission of Nombre de Dios. Again in 1735 the same Colonel returned, reinforced and avid to win this new land from the Spaniards. But his second attempt failed, and the officer of King George was killed among the shards of the statue his men had desecrated. Religion was not the issue; this was a clash of nations for control of territory, in the course of which Christian work had to suffer.

In 1740 the English General Oglethorpe laid siege to St. Augustine's, and, although unsuccessful, his attack was so terrifying as almost to wipe out the Mission. Spanish Florida, the land of flowers, next became a pawn, and the territory passed to the British in 1763 in a "peaceful bargain"; it served as a ransom for the return of Cuba to the Spanish. Twenty years later Florida was bartered back to the Spanish by the British in return for possession of Gibraltar.

First Baptist Church, Providence, Rhode Island
(photo by Norman S. Watson)

But the Spanish were not bold enough or strong enough to hold the territory. So eventually, while the British promised the Catholics religious freedom "so far as the laws of Great Britain permit," the Spaniards took refuge in Cuba. Perhaps the promise of religious freedom was looked upon with a skeptical eye; at any rate, the wary Spaniards departed. Yet the Mission remains and today is a place of pilgrimage.

The Spaniards had very likely been hesitant to believe the British promise because they knew that the north was being settled in great numbers by individuals fleeing religious persecution in Europe. But history tells us of these new settlers that they were tenacious, resolved, and that they set up their churches with the intention of remaining.

One of the early leaders of those seeking freedom of worship was Roger Williams. His mark upon the new land remains a great historic achievement. The First Baptist Church in America, now a stately colonial landmark, is the oldest church of any denomination in the State of Rhode Island, and the oldest Baptist church in America. It was founded in 1639, shortly after Williams and his followers had settled the city of Providence, and has maintained a continuous existence from that time.

The first Rhode Island settlers under the leadership of Roger Williams, their minister, came from Salem, from which place he had been banished two years before. Others had joined them from Boston, and here, on land they purchased from the Indians, they founded a colony in which they themselves might enjoy, and also offer to all men "distressed of conscience," the priceless boon of soul-liberty. For the first time in the history of the world a state was to be founded with civil and religious liberty as its cornerstone.

The present church is located on an acre-and-a-quarter tract of land, and is the third building constructed since its

Old North Church, Boston, Massachusetts

founding. This building was begun in 1774 and dedicated in 1775, midway between the battles of Lexington and Bunker Hill. As a specimen of colonial architecture it is unsurpassed. It has a seating capacity of eight hundred on the main floor and six hundred in the gallery. The spire, 185 feet high, is most beautiful; it is a close copy of one of the many proposed but not used designs of a steeple for St. Martin's-in-the-fields in London. The body of the building is essentially that of Marybone Chapel, both being of the Sir Christopher Wren type, and delineated by James Gibbs, a pupil of that celebrated church builder.

The First Baptist Church exemplifies the social and civic use to which some of the early church buildings were put by the settlers. Built with a large seating capacity for that time, it has served the community on many occasions for gatherings of national or state importance. It has also, except for one or two years, housed the Brown University commencements. James Manning was simultaneously the first president of Brown University and minister of the First Baptist Church when its Meeting House was built. It was therefore dedicated "For the Publick Worship of Almighty God, and also for holding Commencement in."

There was a quaint inscription on the original bell that hung in the Meeting House steeple. This bell, weighing 2,500 pounds, was made in London, and bore the lines:

> For freedom of conscience the town was first planted,
> Persuasion, not force, was used by the people:
> This Church is the eldest, and has not recanted,
> Enjoying and granting bell, temple and steeple.

The bell has since been recast, so the inscription has disappeared. The last line, however, bears explanation. Not

Old North Church, Boston, Massachusetts

until after World War I could an English nonconformist religious body in England call its house of worship a church. It was to be called a chapel, and the building could not have a bell or steeple. In the colonies there was no such prohibition —and the bell so declared.

There are probably few American churches which enjoy greater popular distinction than the Old North Church of Boston. This is the city's oldest existing place of worship; its first stone was laid on April 15, 1723. Situated on Salem Street in the vicinity of Copp's Hill, the building was patterned after the style of Sir Christopher Wren, and remains essentially unchanged today. Only its pulpit, pews, and desk are of more recent date, and some renovations have been necessary to repair damages wrought by time and the elements. The steeple was torn off by Hurricane Carol in 1954, but has since been replaced in its original beauty by public subscription.

The tower of this Puritan Episcopal church is a colonial gem, and contains a chime of eight bells, one of which bears the inscription: "The first ring cast for the British empire in North America, 1744." The tower has other distinctions. An old newsletter of 1757 narrates how one John Childs gave notice that he would perform by "flying" from the steeple of "Dr. Cutler's Church," and did so, descending on a rigged rope. The feat satisfactorily performed before a "great number of spectators" was repeated with the added fillip that John Childs this time set off on his flying descent with two loaded pistols and discharged them in his flight. Such goings-on were considered unseemly by the religious-minded—and besides, such performances kept "people from their place of business." So he was forbidden to do more "flying in the Town." He seems to have bowed to that early "watch and ward" restriction, because he did cease to perform.

*Old South Meeting House, Boston, Massachusetts
(photo by Shaw Studios)*

Much more seriously and significantly, it was from the steeple of Old North Church that the signal lanterns were hung that sent Paul Revere on his countryside-rousing ride. As a boy, Paul Revere, famed worker in metal, had been one of the bell-ringers at the church. The story of his famous ride is told by Dr. Henry Burroughs in this manner: "The signal lanterns of Paul Revere from the church steeple announced the beginning of those hostilities which ended in the establishment of the independence of the United States. It was suspected that Gen. Gage was preparing an expedition to Concord to capture the stores and ammunition collected there by the Americans; and Dr. Joseph Warren remained in Boston, while the Provincial Congress was in session at Concord, to watch the movements of the British, and communicate them to Hancock and Adams, who were attending the Congress, and were staying at the house of Rev. Jonas Clark in Lexington. On the 15th of April, there were discovered signs of an early movement of the troops; and Paul Revere by Dr. Warren's request rode to Lexington, and gave notice to the patriots. On his return it occurred to him that when it should become necessary to send word that the British were actually on the march, it might be impossible for a messenger to leave Boston; and so he agreed with Col. Conant and other friends whom he saw in Charlestown, that—in his own words—'if the British went out by water we would show two lanterns in the North Church steeple, and if by land one, as a signal.' When it was found on the evening of the 18th that the troops were preparing to cross from Boston in boats, Revere went to the North end, made his preparation, and was rowed with muffled oars under the guns of a British vessel to the Charlestown shore."

The height of the tower, built from a design by Charles Bulfinch, and the weather conditions contributed toward

Old South Church in Boston, Boston, Massachusetts
(Lenscraft Photos, Inc.)

making the signal clearly visible. The historic event of the Revere warning is commemorated in a tablet erected on the front of the Church in 1878.

The third, and present, Old South Church, in use since 1875, is located in Copley Square. Its antecedents, however, have given this old Congregational church its place in our nation's history. The congregation was founded and the first church erected in 1669; it was then known as the Third Church in Boston. Liberal in its membership requirements, it has been hailed as a starting wedge in the separation of church and state in our land.

It was the second church, built in 1729, the famous Old South Meeting House, that won a unique role in history. This building still stands on Washington Street in Boston, hearkening back to the time when our forefathers suffered the injustice of taxation without representation. Here many pre-revolutionary meetings were held, and here was laid the daring, whimsical, but effective plan for the Boston Tea Party. It was here that Benjamin Franklin was baptized when he was twenty-four hours old; here leaders of clergy and laity prayed as they prepared to lead a new nation in national, political, and educational activities. Old South Church is the owner of the famous Thomas Prince Library, the Reverend Prince being a colonial minister of the church. Now, for reasons of preservation, this notable collection of colonial Americana is housed in the Boston Public Library. Much of the collection was destroyed by British soldiers during the Revolution, when they gathered volumes each day from the tower of the Meeting House to light the fires in the church, which had been turned into a riding academy. Even so, twenty-seven hundred volumes and pamphlets remain today, including two copies of the celebrated Bay Psalm Book, the first book printed in America, and considered the most valuable book printed in English.

The present congregation attends a Forefathers' Day Service at the Old Meeting House on the Sunday following Thanksgiving each year. The present church is noted for its windows, made in England of seventeenth-century glass, and for its mosaics over the entrance. These were acquired from an early Eastern Church which later became a Moslem mosque.

In 1954 the Reformed Protestant Dutch Church of Flatbush celebrated its Tercentennial. Organized in 1654, it has served continuously since that year when, by order of Governor Peter Stuyvesant, it was erected at its present site, Flatbush and Church Avenues. By present-day standards its cost was modest—only eighteen hundred dollars, a sum to which the Governor personally contributed. This original building was the first church erected in the area (then the Town of Flatbush), and the present church site is the oldest in Greater New York.

The second building was erected in 1699. At the time of the American Revolution its bell gave warning of the approach of the British who, during the Battle of Long Island, had effected a landing from Staten Island on August 22, 1776.

In 1796 the present church building was constructed, with a colonial tower and belfry. The present bell, donated at the time by the Honorable John Vanderbilt, was captured by the British on its way from Holland, and carried to Halifax. From there it was brought to Flatbush and hung in the belfry, where it has tolled the death of every President of the United States from George Washington on. The church was most recently renovated in 1926.

Amid the strife and struggle of founding a new nation,

some warmly human events have come well into the foreground historically. Such an event is associated with St. Peter's Church of New Kent County, Virginia, an Episcopal edifice which has come to be known as "The first church of the first First Lady."

Construction on historic St. Peter's Church was begun in 1701 and completed in 1703. The building was erected about forty miles from Richmond on the Pomunky River, on an estate which came to be known as the "Washington estate" because George Washington became associated with it through his marriage to Mrs. Martha Custis, and lived there at the "White House" for a short time after his marriage, before moving to Mount Vernon. The church was built at a cost of 164,000 pounds of tobacco, then the accepted currency of the locality. Its steeple was erected twelve years later.

The architectural style of the church is simple, pleasing Old English; this is one of the most attractive colonial churches of Virginia still standing. The following quaint account is that traditionally given of the marriage of our first President on January 6, 1759: "Washington and Mrs. Custis rode to the Church in a gorgeous chariot, and the invited persons followed them in vehicles of various shapes. When they stood up before the minister to be married, Washington towered beside his betrothed, who looked unusually small and low in stature; and the difference was remarked by all who were present. Washington was in uniform, and Mrs. Custis was arrayed in a fine white-silk dress. As they came out of the Church, the newly united couple had a joyful appearance, Washington himself smiling upon and chatting with several of the attendants. All the servants on the White House estate were given a holiday, and all in holiday attire joined in the general merry-making that followed."

The "White House" estate was the home of Martha Wash-

opposite: Reformed Protestant Dutch Church of Flatbush, Brooklyn, New York   (Acker Photo Service)

ington, as the widow of Daniel Parke Custis. In 1757 the property descended to her son, John Parke Custis, and upon his death in 1781, it went to *his* son, George Washington Parke Custis, who was then six months old. Also in 1781, George Washington Parke Custis and his sister, Nelly Custis, were adopted by the Washingtons, and from that time until 1804 these adopted children made their home at Mount Vernon. The only child of George Washington Parke Custis, Mary Ann Randolph Custis, married Robert E. Lee in 1821.

The church itself was the scene of important military activity during the Civil War. General Lee, who continued an interest in the church and gave it substantial financial support, records that during hostilities St. Peter's was used as a stable by the Federal Cavalry, with much damage to the windows and interior. To the great General this defacement must have been an added sorrow.

In 1957 copies of the famous Gilbert Stuart portraits of George Washington and Martha Washington, done by Joseph T. Harris in 1835, were presented to the St. Peter's Church restoration as a part of Virginia's three hundred and fiftieth anniversary celebration. St. Peter's, still in use, is being preserved as a historic monument.

When the notes of that new-world sound, religious freedom, began to echo through the world in the seventeenth century, many diverse peoples heard it. Among them was a group of fifteen Spanish-Portuguese Jews who promptly set out to seek the liberty promised in the declaration issued by Roger Williams. This group came to Newport, in what now is the State of Rhode Island, and there founded Congregation Jeshuat Israel in 1658.

For a little more than a century the Jews of Newport held their religious services in private homes. Then, on December

*Touro Synagogue, Newport, Rhode Island
(photo by J. Gilbert Harrington)*

2, 1763, after four years of construction, Touro Synagogue was dedicated to its holy purpose. It was the first synagogue built here, and has remained in continuous use ever since. Designed by the architect Peter Harrison, who also designed the Redwood Library and the Brick Market in Newport, it is a fine colonial structure. The designer was an amateur in many respects who served freely, without payment, garnering his information from books. But he built well, with a sense of proportion and harmony which led Fiske Kimball to declare this synagogue to be "one of the most perfect works in colonial architecture." Notable among its features is a gallery supported by twelve Ionic columns, above which are twelve Corinthian columns supporting the domed ceiling. Five massive hand-wrought bronze candelabra were presented as memorial gifts in the ten years after its dedication; and the Scrolls of the Law within the Ark are antiquities of great beauty.

Touro Synagogue is rich in the kind of historical associations which made our early houses of worship the practical as well as spiritual bulwarks of a new nation. It was in this building that the Rhode Island General Assembly met in 1780 and the State Supreme Court held sessions, and here that a town meeting was held when George Washington visited Newport in 1781. When President Washington came to Newport again nine years later, Moses Seixas, the warden, addressed the President and elicited from him this famous declaration: "For happily, the Government of the United States which gives to bigotry no sanction, to persecution no assistance, requires only that they who live under its protection should demean themselves as good citizens, in giving it on all occasions their effectual support."

Though the Jewish community virtually disappeared in the hard years following the Revolution, in which many of its

Touro Synagogue, Newport, Rhode Island
(photo by J. Gilbert Harrington)

members fought, the synagogue retained its identity as a Sephardic synagogue in the succeeding centuries. In its cemetery are buried many of its founders. At the time of its dedication, the spiritual leader of the congregation was the Rabbi Isaac Touro, for whom the synagogue was named. He was the father of Judah Touro, who became one of the great philanthropists of the United States. Judah Touro endowed the first free library on this continent, and probably in the world; he helped to complete the Bunker Hill Monument, and he made generous gifts, during his lifetime and in his will, to every type of charitable and welfare agency, without regard to creed or color. The Touro Infirmary, the famous hospital in New Orleans, is named for him. He is buried in the cemetery of Touro Synagogue.

Surrounded by this aura of history and service, Touro Synagogue is the first Jewish house of worship to be designated a National Historic Site by the National Parks Service of the Department of the Interior. Speaking at the dedication ceremony on August 31, 1947, the historian Carl Van Doren said: "There can be no great nations without faithful memories of great deeds and great thoughts. If nations cherish unworthy memories from their past they will perform unworthy actions in the present and be satisfied with unworthy hopes for the future. But when, as this afternoon, a generation honors a shrine long consecrated to justice and holiness, that generation does honor to the best in itself as well as to the shrine."

While the English colonies in America increased steadily in number and strength, allegiance to the mother country was nevertheless sustained for a century. The churches reflected this allegiance, for colonial authorities were church-minded and actively fostered the Anglican faith.

When, after the Revolutionary War, the parishes of the

Trinity Church, New York City (photo by Myron S. Shepard)

Church of England in this country were organized into the Protestant Episcopal Church of America, Trinity Church of New York was a recognized leader. William III of England had founded this church by a Royal Charter in 1697. It is today the oldest Episcopal church in the city. The present structure is the third to be erected on the original site, and was designed by Richard Upjohn.

"Old Trinity's" street address, Wall Street and Broadway, records two of the earliest landmarks on Manhattan Island. Broadway began as hardly more than a cowpath, which widened with use into the Broad Way. Wall Street follows the line of the wall or stockade built by the Dutch settlers in 1653 at the northern edge of the town, and extended along Rector Street twenty years later. In 1664 the British, who laid claim to the whole Atlantic seaboard, took Nieuw Amsterdam from the Dutch and renamed the city New York, after the Duke of York, brother of King Charles II of England.

With the English came the Church of England, at first represented by military chaplains and later, as their following grew, by community churches. Later, more lasting structures were established to serve regular parishes. For nearly a century, Trinity Parish was the only Church of England parish on Manhattan Island. As the population continued to increase, two chapels were erected to provide services: St. George's in 1752 and St. Paul's in 1766. (St. George's became an independent parish in 1811.) By the original charter and a 1705 bequest known as Queen Anne's Grant, Trinity Church has, with its rich patrimony of land, been able to make handsome gifts to every kind of religious and social work down through the years.

The early church left a permanent stamp upon the city, for numerous streets in lower Manhattan were named for early rectors and vestrymen, such as Vesey, Barclay, Moore, and Charlton.

St. Paul's Chapel, New York City   (photo by Frank Cleveland)

During the early days of the American Revolution, George Washington and his troops occupied New York, and it was at Trinity Church that the General attended services. The first church building, however, was destroyed in the great fire of September 21, 1776, and the ruins of Trinity became known as the "Burnt Church"; the congregation continued services at St. Paul's Chapel. The second church on the site of Trinity was consecrated on March 25, 1790, and George Washington sat in a specially-canopied pew during the services. After the Revolution, Trinity Church, with confirmation of its charter by the State of New York, passed without untoward incident from the status of an English colonial parish to that of an American parish. The third and present building was consecrated on May 21, 1846.

Trinity Church contains many treasures of art and workmanship. In its tower are some of the oldest church bells in this country, the first of which was brought over in 1797 on the ship *Favorite*. There are now ten bells, the largest weighing 3,000 pounds, and their sound echoes through the financial district as it did in the nineteenth century when, by order of the Mayor, the bells pealed out fire alarms. The spire itself served as a landmark to ships at sea until long after the Civil War.

The church is a treasury of memorial gifts. These can still be seen by visitors, and are amply cataloged. But it is the churchyard which gives strongest testimony to Trinity's past. Surrounding the church is the oldest burial ground in lower Manhattan. Here are the graves of Alexander Hamilton, the first Secretary of the Treasury; Robert Fulton, inventor of the steamboat; William Bradford, founder of New York's first newspaper; and many others—heroes, civic leaders, and the unknown faithful. Today the church is a reminder of our first days of freedom, and, appropriately enough, it faces the

St. Paul's Chapel, New York City   (photo by Gottscho-Schleisner)

street where the material fruits of that freedom are counted and marked in ledgers.

First an auxiliary of Trinity Church, St. Paul's Chapel has the distinction of being the oldest public building and sole remaining colonial church on Manhattan Island. The Chapel was authorized in 1763 and dedicated and opened for worship on October 30, 1766. It stands on what had been, at the time of the Chapel's completion, a field outside the city limits. Today this is Greenwich Street.

The building was designed by the architect Thomas Mc-Bean, a Scotsman, and was constructed of native stone, Manhattan mico-schist with quoins of brownstone. It is acclaimed an unexcelled example of Georgian-Classic Revival style, and its woodwork, carvings, and door-hinges are hand wrought. Most of its ornamentation is the work of L'Enfant, French architect and Major of Engineers of the Continental Army of the Revolution, who later laid the plans for the city of Washington, D.C.

The chapel's interior is in many respects a repository of historical memorials and art pieces of unique interest. Above the pulpit can be seen the only emblem of royalty in New York surviving in its original place. This is a carved and gilded coronet and feathers, always a part of the armorial bearings of a Prince of Wales. It represents both the munificence of the Royal House to Trinity parish in earlier times and the association between the Sovereign and the Church of England. On the exterior of the chapel, in a niche above the Broadway Portico, there is an oak statue of St. Paul, a heroic size American primitive, probably carved by the sculptor of the first figurehead of the frigate *Constitution*.

It was to this chapel that President George Washington, immediately following his inauguration, and attended by his cabinet and staff, repaired for an official Service of Thanksgiving. This was in 1789, April 30th, but the President continued to worship here regularly. On the north aisle is the pew, with the initials "G.W." carved on the end, where the President knelt. And here, as a reminder of the struggle which freed us from foreign rule, are the National emblem, the flags of the Continental Army, and the General-in-chief's headquarters flag.

Four of Washington's officers, original members of the Society of Cincinnati, are buried in the churchyard, among civic leaders and great and small men of the eighteenth and nineteenth centuries.

In northeast New Jersey we find a church which began in colonial days and suffered through the days of revolution.

The First Presbyterian Church of Springfield was the achievement of three families who had settled at this historic New Jersey crossroads in 1745. They joined with farmers from the surrounding countryside and put up a log church which for sixteen years served as their center of worship. As their number grew, a second church, larger, more secure, was built as a meeting house in 1761.

But, as occurs at so many crossroads, there was action stirring at Springfield. The movement was on to free the colonies from British domination. Springfield's citizens met, enlisted as patriots, and were so fervent in their support of national freedom that they opened their church to serve as a depot for public stores and supplies for the soldiers. Meanwhile the congregation continued to worship in the garret of the parsonage.

While these patriotic sacrifices were being made, British troops found the crossroads and, during the Battle of Springfield, on June 23, 1780, set fire to the church. It was on that day that, in a quite ironic manner, religious freedom gave support to the cause of freedom in general. The British were marching to Morristown, but were stopped at Springfield. In the pressure of the struggle the patriots were running short of wadding for their guns. Then the pastor of the Elizabeth Presbyterian Church, the Reverend James Caldwell, serving as a chaplain in the Continental Army, rushed into the Springfield church, seized an armful of Hymnals written by Isaac Watts, and gave them to the soldiers, shouting, "Put Watts into them, boys!"

It was not until 1791 that the third and present church was constructed. It, too, is colonial in form, of frame construction. Work and material were contributed by members of the congregation as they were able, for the war had left them poor in more than hymnals. Men came bringing their tools and the best timber their farms could furnish; booths were put up on the grounds, where the women prepared meals for the volunteer workers. It was a community "church raising." Once again, after days of work, the bells were heard again. They can still be heard today, and the church is still known locally as an "Altar of Liberty."

Church expansion progressed westward from the Atlantic seaboard. Between 1769 and 1783, Presbyterian missionaries crossed the Allegheny Mountains to found the first churches of this faith. The Old Stone Church at Lewisburg, West Virginia, was founded in 1783 and erected in 1796. The building is in plain colonial style, with a small bell tower rising from the center of the roof ridge. Its construction was made possible largely through the generosity of Colonel John Stuart, the "Father of Greenbrier County." This church, with its background of extended missionary work, was a strong influence in the early development of this country. It was also

First Presbyterian Church, Springfield, New Jersey

an early leader in education, for it was here in 1812 that Lewisburg Academy was established.

The Old Stone Church is today the oldest unrestored church in continuous use west of the Alleghenies, which is rather remarkable considering its location in the valley around which the battle of Lewisburg was fought in the Civil War. At that time the church served for military use, first as an emergency hospital and later as a billet for troops.

The Spanish conquerors who landed on the western edge of the Gulf of Mexico brought their brown-robed padres with them. Moving inland, these fathers founded the Mission San Antonio de Valero in 1718—the mission more familiarly known as "The Alamo."

Despite the mighty labors of its founders, the Alamo was never to become a great mission center. A hurricane destroyed the first building. The second was erected a short distance away; but sickness, smallpox, and a variety of disasters kept the new foundation from becoming the hoped-for center of conversion. Its records were transferred to the Church of San Fernando in 1793 and, while still incomplete, the Mission of San Antonio lost prestige.

It was not as a religious center that this church was to attain historic stature. In pursuit of their "manifest destiny," Americans were moving into the South and West during the early part of the nineteenth century, encouraged by newspapers and missionary magazines, and lured by the prospect of adventure. Texas, a province of Mexico, was journey's end for many of the immigrants, and this fact stirred President Bustamente of Mexico to forbid further American immigration into Texas. But a formidable number of the free-minded had already arrived, and, under the leadership of Sam Houston, they rose in revolution.

Old Stone Presbyterian Church, Lewisburg, West Virginia

Texas seceded from Mexico in 1835, and at the Alamo the new dictator-president of Mexico, Santa Anna, destroyed the entire garrison of 183 Texans who, fighting under the leadership of W. B. Travis, occupied the Mission as a fort. The rallying cry became, "Remember the Alamo!" Spurred partly by the war-cry, and partly by the knowledge that a heavy toll had been taken of the Mexican forces, the Texans were victorious at San Jacinto on April 21, 1836. From then until it entered the Union in 1845, Texas was an independent republic.

Thus the Mission of San Antonio became known as the Cradle of Texas, and remains, not as a church, but as a place sacred to the cause of freedom.

There were problems to be faced before the consolidation of America could be achieved. Among many earlier, perhaps statelier churches, one stands out because of its association with the only President of the Confederate States during the years of the Civil War. The Church of the Redeemer at Biloxi, Mississippi, was founded in 1858, and the first church, now the parish house, was built in 1874. The present church building was erected in 1891.

In this Episcopal church the pew of Jefferson Davis, the Confederate President, and his family is marked by a draped Confederate flag and a silver plate. It was to this church that he went during the years he lived at Beauvoir; the church was supported by the Davis family for years afterward. To this church also came many famous Confederate soldiers: General Stewart and Brigadier General Ferguson, who had received the keys of surrender of Fort Sumter. While the Church of the Redeemer was not to figure in historic actions, it stands today as a link to the past, when we were divided, and as a center of living faith in a now united land.

II

MISSION CHURCHES ACROSS THE LAND

Missions and missionary activity in the United States make a subject of challenging proportions. The span of time encompassed by mission enterprise has been given as 1567 to 1861, but this period embraces chiefly the Indian missions. Church expansion in membership by any denomination may be looked upon as mission activity, however, and thus the term cannot properly be limited to the conversion of native inhabitants. We can see that as the New World was opened up by discovery and settlement and later by its success as an independent nation of united and sovereign states, there were two mission fields. The first comprised the natives, the second the church groups themselves, to accommodate increasing numbers of settlers.

In the latter sense all church building may be considered "mission activity," and this continues even to the present time, when church membership is steadily growing. Also missionary work among American Indians, and other activity directed toward the conversion of non-church peoples, goes on apace.

We can therefore see that the mission churches have followed two distinct patterns of operation, the first tied in with settlement and the conversion of the natives, and the second following the lines of nationality and migration patterns of people moving from east to west across the country and settling in usually homogeneous communities.

Almost from the first settlement of the territory of the New World there was concern and concerted effort made toward Christianizing the Indians. The first such move by the Spaniards, following along the conquest routes of the explorers, was to establish permanent settlements of Spanish families and religious leaders among the natives. This was done chiefly in the South and Southwest. Since Spain is a Catholic country, the missions established were Catholic. The French Jesuit missions which followed the route along the St. Lawrence and Great Lakes seaway were also Catholic, but these were not as successful as the Spanish missions of the Southwest. Working in the Northeast, under the aegis of the French government, the Jesuits found it difficult to set up permanent missions that could survive.

On the New England coast the Puritan, Episcopalian, Presbyterian, Baptist, Congregational, and Moravian groups were also developing permanent settlements. Frequently written into their land grants was the condition that the grantees extend their efforts to the conversion of the natives. This resulted in some concerted effort being made toward Christianizing the inland tribes, although here the lack of trained personnel was a limiting factor. However, the matter of conversions was taken more than seriously, and from the Congregational mission at Martha's Vineyard in 1643 to the 1861 Lutheran mission to the Indians about Cheyenne, Wyoming, hundreds of native missions were established by some twenty denominations.

In the second phase of missionary activity, that of church expansion, we see a growth which encompassed the nationalities that immigrated and began the westward trek. The "missionary" nature of these churches is evident in the fact that they received financial support from the people of England, Germany, or France. The Anglican Church of England supported many of our early churches, if not in funds, then in such material ways as giving "silver services," "vessels," and "rings of bells." Catholic groups in the United States benefited greatly by donations, in the thousands of dollars, from such missionary groups as the "Ludwigsmissionverein of Munich" and the "Leopoldinen Stiftung of Vienna."

What the historian Doctor Bolton wrote of Spanish missions, we might say of all mission churches. In effect, he said that a distinct feature of any mission church is that in ceasing to be a "mission" in the true sense of the word, it either becomes a permanent church or fits itself into an altered role. The fact that a mission has served to raise a native response to religion and initiate the building of permanent or more lasting structures of religion is proof of the mission's success.

For the sake of order we have chosen to present first the Spanish missions of the South and Southwest. They are notable not only as religious achievements, but also because they introduced ideas on architecture and irrigation which have influenced the pattern of building in this country. We shall touch on only a few of these missions, for they have been extensively treated in other, more special, works. The Spaniards were not only intrepid in the matter of founding missions, but we marvel at their physical industry in founding so many of them.

The Spanish missioners used all the systems of construction

that had been developed up to their time. Considering the limitations of material, the lack of machinery, and the necessity of training the natives before they could build, it is surprising that these mission churches were so influential architecturally. Three notable structural systems were used by the Spaniards in this early mission period. While these were well enough known at the time, in mission building they were unique. The three types of framework were the post and lintel, the arch and pier, and the truss. Employed with adobe and the unfinished timbers available, they made for strong, and, for the climate, quite lasting construction.

The decorative details are also noteworthy. The open belltower with the bell swinging freely in the open niche was characteristic and is used today in some of our modern church buildings. Similarly, the *bovedas,* the masonry domes, were an innovation and a marked contrast with the octagonal, square, and pointed towers of colonial churches by Bulfinch and others.

The Spanish mission architecture had considerable influence on American building in the Southwest. It was in itself derivative, developed from the Roman, Moorish, Spanish-Gothic, and the Plateresque, which, in turn, was borrowed from Italy and was characterized by the highly ornate, as seen in the surface decoration about the doorways of some missions. These features of the Spanish missions have contributed to a single style and given rise to the Spanish-colonial architecture in vogue on the Pacific coast. Briefly, these features are: solid, massive walls and buttresses; arches carried on piers and curved pedimented gables; terraced bell towers with lantern; pierced or windowed walls or towers; the patio with fountain or garden; broad, undecorated walls; projecting or overhanging eaves and low-pitched, red-tiled roofs.

The history of the missions of the South and Southwest is in itself a fascinating study, but we can be sure that sand,

San Xavier del Bac, near Tucson, Arizona
(photo by "Frashers," Pomona, California)

thirst, the broiling sun, and the threat of death were less romantic than our backward glance tends to make them appear.

NEW MEXICO

The first expeditions of the Spaniards, those of Coronado and Espejo in the sixteenth century, were military and for the purpose of exploration. But where the explorers went, missionaries followed. In 1598, when Don Juan de Oñate led his expedition into what is now the State of New Mexico, he brought with him a large following of settlers, seven thousand head of cattle, and ten Franciscan friars.

Rather boastfully, in keeping with the style of the period, he declared his intention. In part he said: "I wish that those that are now, or at any time may be, know that I, Don Juan de Oñate, [am] governor and captain general, and Adelantado of New Mexico, and of its kingdoms and provinces, as well as of those in their vicinity and contiguous thereto, as settler, discoverer and pacifier of them and of the said kingdoms, by the order of the King, our Lord. I find myself today with my full and entire camp near the river which they call Del Norte, and on the bank which is contiguous to the first towns of New Mexico, and whereas I wish to take possession of the land today, the day of the Ascension of our Lord, dated April 30th, of the present year 1598, through the medium of the person of Don Juan Perez de Donis, clerk of his Majesty, and secretary of this expedition and the government of said kingdoms and provinces, by authority and in the name of the most Christian King, Don Felipe, Segundo, and for his successors . . ."

From this beginning there were to be erected in New Mexico no less than twenty-four missions. Many of these are in ruins, but others remain as memorials of a zealous effort to advance the cause of Christianity. Rapidly the base of opera-

tion moved from the first established capital at San Gabriel
to Sante Fe in 1605, and in the report of Benavides it was
stated of the new capital: "It only lacked the principal thing,
which was the church; that which they had being a poor
'jacal,' because the Friars attended first to the building of the
churches for the Indians whom they had converted, and with
whom they lived; and so as soon as I became Custodio I began to construct the Church and convento to the honor and
glory of God."

Thus, after the religious obligation to the Indians had been
attended to, the church of San Miguel was erected for the
settlers. It was built on the old Sante Fe Trail, and measured
some seventy feet long and twenty-five feet wide. The walls
were adobe, five feet thick, and battlemented on top. The
original mission remains, though much repaired. It is a place
filled with strange, beautiful relics of the early missions. In
the tower was hung the already historic 780-pound bell cast
in Spain in 1356 and inscribed "St. Joseph, pray for us." It
is felt, traditionally, that this bell rang out the birth of Christianity in Mexico and above the Rio Grande just as it had
sounded the knell of Islam in Spain a century before.

In Sante Fe stands the Cathedral of Saint Francis, facing
the plaza of this early settlement. Although founded in 1610,
the first church of the name built in the city of "Holy Faith"
was built by Benavides in 1627, nearly destroyed in the
Pueblo Revolution of 1680, and rebuilt in 1713. It stood until
the present Cathedral, constructed in 1866 in the early mission pattern, was built by John Baptist Lamy, the first desert
bishop. In her book, *Death Comes for the Archbishop,* the
novelist Willa Cather was writing of this church and this
bishop. The present building was finished, except for its
intended steeples, in 1866. Its towers have remained steeple-
less, but with no loss of beauty to the Cathedral's setting

today, against the modern skyline and the Sangre de Cristo Mountains in the distance.

The State of Texas, which has progressed through the stages of a province of Mexico and independent republic, and is to-day the largest of the United States, has a history of sprawling mission activity. The Spaniards started out along the Rio Grande River and established seven missions in what was then known as the Paso Del Norte valley. Owing to the shift-ing of the Rio Grande and its establishment as the boundary between the United States and Mexico after the end of the war in 1848, three of the original missions were left south of the border. Missionary progression now turned northward, and a series of seven missions was established by the Span-iards, chiefly around what is now the city of San Antonio.

Texas records the first episcopal authority on the continen-tal United States with the appointment in 1527 of a bishop-elect, Juan Suarez, O.F.M., to the territory then known as Provincia del Rio Panuco y Victoria Garayana. Religious ser-vices were held in what is now El Paso by Reverend Fray Augustin Rodriguez, O.F.M. as early as 1578.

We shall consider only one of these missions of Texas, the one called the "Mother Mission," which in 1952 celebrated its two hundred and seventy-first birthday. Originally known as "Misión de Corpus Christi de la Ysleta del Sur," it was later renamed "Misión de San Antonio de las Tiguas." After 1881 the Mission was given its present name of Nuestra Señora del Monte Carmel.

Mount Carmel Mission was founded in 1682 to serve as a refuge for the Tiguas Indians. Its founders were Fray Fran-cisco Ayeta, O.F.M., and the New Mexico Governor, Don Antonio Otermin. The Mission served its purpose well, for